PELICAN BOOKS

A822

INDUSTRY IN THE U.S.A.

Geoffrey Owen was born in Wiltshire in 1934 and educated at Rugby School and Oxford, where he read Greats and won a 'blue' for both tennis and hockey. From 1956 to 1958 he served as an education officer in the R.A.F. and then joined the staff of the *Financial Times*, subsequently to become an industrial correspondent. In 1961 he became the paper's U.S. correspondent and moved to New York, where he stayed until the end of 1964. He returned to London to become Industrial Editor of the *Financial Times*.

While in the United States, Geoffrey Owen travelled widely and covered the economic, industrial and political news with special emphasis on large industrial companies. Back in England, he is more concerned with the general question of how to make British industry more effective and successful.

Geoffrey Owen is married with two children and lives in Wimbledon.

GEOFFREY OWEN

INDUSTRY IN THE U.S.A.

PENGUIN BOOKS
BALTIMORE · MARYLAND

Penguin Books Ltd, Harmondsworth, Middlesex, England
Penguin Books Inc., 3300 Clipper Mill Road, Baltimore 11, Md, U.S.A.
Penguin Books Pty Ltd, Ringwood, Victoria, Australia

—

First published 1966

Copyright © Geoffrey Owen, 1966

—

Made and printed in Great Britain
by C. Nicholls & Company Ltd, Manchester
Set in Monotype Times

Contents

Tables

Introduction

THE American businessman enjoys a worldwide reputation for efficiency. For more than a hundred years visitors from overseas have inspected American factories and interviewed American managers, seeking lessons which could be applied in their own countries. Today, when competition is more international than ever before, other countries are beginning to catch up with the United States. The gap is being narrowed, partly because American methods have been adopted more extensively in other countries. But there is still a widespread and probably well-founded belief that, in the management of private industry, the average standard of efficiency is higher in the United States than elsewhere. It is not clear whether this difference is due to more enterprising managers, a more adaptable labour force, a larger and more competitive home market, or other factors; it is unlikely that any single explanation will suffice.

The admiration of foreigners is not confined to the businessman. The American economic system has been studied as a model, or at least as a source of ideas which can be profitably borrowed and applied elsewhere. In Britain at the present time, when the need to improve the performance of the economy is urgent, there is considerable interest – among businessmen, trade union leaders, and government officials – in the American approach to economic and industrial problems. The purpose of this book is to contribute to a clearer understanding of American industry and of the reasons for its success.

It is, of course, quite wrong to assume that the American approach is always superior to our own. The Americans, after all, have been far from satisfied with their economic performance in recent years. Until very recently their rate of growth has been sluggish in comparison to the spectacular advance of such countries as Germany and Japan; they, too, have looked overseas for policies which could be borrowed and adapted for use in the United States. There are even signs in the United States of the same mood of national self-criticism which has become so prevalent in Britain.

Most of the advanced industrial countries have similar economic objectives, of which full employment without inflation is the most fundamental. The United States has been no more successful than Britain in combining full employment with stable prices. In the first half of the current decade the Americans enjoyed price stability, but only at the cost of substantial unemployment. By the beginning of 1966 unemployment had at last been reduced to somewhere near an acceptable level, but there were signs of another outbreak of inflation, aggravated by the artificial stimulus of the war in Vietnam. Thus, as this book goes to press, the Americans are grappling once again with the problem which is familiar in Britain – how to maintain a full-employment economy without letting prices and wages get out of control.

Similarly, many of the specific industrial problems which are much discussed in the U.K. – how to speed up the docks, how to streamline the railway system, how to help the textile industry compete against imports, how to modernize the building industry, how to eliminate restrictive practices among the trade unions, how to make the labour force more mobile – have their counterparts in the United States. The performance of the steel industry is almost as hot a political issue in the United States as it is in Britain. In both countries the relationships between government and industry, government and labour, industry and labour, are being re-examined.

Britain's problems are not unique. But Britain can learn from studying how similar problems are being tackled in the United States, from examining where the Americans are succeeding and where they are failing, what advantages or disadvantages they possess in their traditions, institutions and attitudes. This book examines the performance of American industry and the various factors which influence it – competition, government policy, the power of the trade unions, the demands of shareholders and the financial community. It considers the framework of law and tradition in which the American businessman operates.

Most of the material for the book was obtained between 1961

and the end of 1964, when the author was resident in the United States as Correspondent for the *Financial Times*. In addition to the wealth of published information, the freedom with which American businessmen and public officials discuss their problems with members of the Press (including the foreign Press) has been extremely valuable in the preparation of the book.

*

Any attempt to understand American industry is complicated by the persistence of slogans, notably about the proper role of government in economic affairs, which usually reflect the prejudices of particular interest groups, but which are sometimes regarded as facts. The first chapter attempts to set in perspective the relative importance of business and government in promoting American prosperity.

Vigorous internal competition has always been a central feature of the American economy, and one of the reasons for the superior efficiency of American industry. This is the subject of Chapter 2. Recent developments in the economy, including the growth of imports, have tended to sharpen the pressure of competition. The seller's market of the early postwar period has given way to a situation of severe competition, in which marketing has assumed a crucial importance for almost every industry.

As competition grows more intense, so businessmen are inclined to find new ways of evading it. Through the antitrust laws the Federal Government has tried to maintain competition, eliminate price-fixing and curb the trend towards mergers and amalgamations. The advantages and limitations of America's tough anti-monopoly legislation are discussed in Chapter 3.

In some sectors of industry, such as transport, energy and communications, the antitrust laws have had to be supplemented or replaced by Government regulation. These are the so-called natural monopolies where technological or economic factors prevent the existence of more than one or a few firms in each market. In these industries, which in other countries are often owned by the government, the responsibility of management is shared between private businessmen and public officials. The unsatisfactory results of this division are discussed in Chapter 4.

The modern business corporation is, typically, owned by a large number of stockholders. Often there is no single individual or institution with more than one per cent of the total shares outstanding. The stockholders make demands on the company's management which have to be met. 'Making money for the stockholders' is sometimes said to be the manager's primary objective. The relations between management and the shareholder are examined in Chapter 5.

Another important group which has claims on the company is its labour force. Most companies have to negotiate over wages and working conditions with trade unions. The power of the unions, their impact on management, and new developments in collective bargaining are discussed in Chapter 6.

Although management is not yet a science, the application of reason to management problems has been growing; the 'intuitive' manager is often said to be on the wane. The rise of the business schools and the management consultants, the development of a professional approach towards management, are discussed in Chapter 7.

Two spheres of activity in which the professional manager is increasingly interested – the financing of scientific research and the growth of overseas investment – are examined in Chapters 8 and 9. In the first, the Government, largely through the space and defence programmes, has become a very important partner. As for the second, the emergence of powerful corporations operating in several different countries is creating new problems both for the managers and for the governments of the countries where they do business.

In Chapter 10 the question of economic growth is considered. Full employment without inflation, a faster rate of economic growth, balance of payments equilibrium – to achieve these objectives, in the United States as well as in Britain, a new combination of public and private policies is needed. Recent developments in business–Government cooperation may have contributed to the improved performance of the American economy.

Finally in Chapter 11 the role of the businessman in American society is assessed. It has often been said that America is a business civilization, that the interests of businessmen take precedence over those of society as a whole. But there are signs that a new generation of businessmen is emerging, more pragmatic and less doctrinaire in its attitudes than in the past. The influence of business on the quality of American society will always be great, but, under the leadership of the new generation, the contribution of the business community to the solution of America's social and political problems, both at home and overseas, may be more constructive and intelligent than it has been in the past.

1 · Business and Government

THE calibre of American businessmen has always impressed foreign observers as a major reason for America's economic success. There is, of course, no single explanation for America's achievements. A number of factors are probably responsible, including her geographical isolation, the newness of American society and the absence of feudalism, her immense resources of land and raw materials. A shortage of skilled labour in the early nineteenth century may have forced American manufacturers to mechanize their factories and invest in labour-saving equipment more rapidly than their foreign counterparts.[1] At the same time, they had the advantage of a large, rapidly growing and homogeneous home market, which was a stimulus to standardization and mass production. But it is also likely that the values of American society were unusually conducive to vigorous business performance.

'The American', wrote de Tocqueville, 'is devoured by the longing to make his fortune; it is the unique passion of his life. Everyone here wants to grow rich and rise in the world, and there is no one but believes in his power to succeed in that'.[2] Social attitudes in the U.S. have tended to favour business as a career for men of talent and initiative; it has generally ranked above government service, the professions, and the army – occupations which in other countries have attracted much of the best talent. In the absence of a hereditary class system (except for a modest bias in favour of 'white Anglo-Saxon protestants'), class status is related almost entirely to income, which in turn depends on occupational achievement, on success in one's job. Newcomers, especially immigrants, have had to fight hard for advancement, but the possibility of 'making good' is real. The belief in an open avenue to wealth, reinforced by the Puritan gospel of hard work, has encouraged a more favourable attitude to entrepreneurship, money-making and risk-taking than in less egalitarian societies.

15

Relations between employer and employee have been as violent and bitter in the U.S. as anywhere in the world. But there has never been the ideological gulf between the two sides which has existed, and still exists, in many other countries. While there has been an undercurrent of hostility to 'big business', especially strong in the 1890s and the 1920s when irresponsible and extravagant behaviour by businessmen aroused deep resentment, socialist ideas have made much less headway in the U.S. than in Western Europe and consequently there is less contempt for the 'profit motive' approach to economic activity. The picture of America as the land of individual opportunity is often overstated (many Americans, like the Negroes and other minority groups, have had very little chance for advancement), but there is a significant degree of equality of opportunity and mobility between classes. There is also, perhaps, a spirit of individual optimism which encourages Americans to set high goals for themselves and to pursue them energetically. All this has a favourable influence on the motivation and performance of American businessmen.

Partly because of the prestige of business as a career, the study of business has been carried out more carefully and more systematically in the U.S. than anywhere else. While America's contributions to basic scientific knowledge may be smaller, in relation to her population, than those of some other countries, her record of contributions to 'managerial' knowledge has been unmatched. In part this reflects the work of institutions like the Harvard Business School, which have provided not only training for businessmen, but also facilities for the study of business activity. From this study has emerged, not the 'science' of management that may once have been hoped for, but an ever-growing body of knowledge and experience which can be applied to concrete business situations. The business schools have contributed to an atmosphere in which the application of reason and knowledge to business problems – in budgeting, marketing, purchasing, labour relations and so on – is accepted by businessmen as necessary and valuable. Innovation in managerial techniques is almost as important as technological innovation, and the United States continues to be a prolific source of new ideas in this field.

The skill and energy of the businessman have been supplemented by the activities of the Federal Government. Reluctant though some businessmen are to admit it, the Government has played an important role in stimulating America's industrial and economic development. Historically, the division of responsibilities between government and business has been worked out on a pragmatic basis. In the field of transport, for example, Government funds have been used to build railways, roads, canals, aeroplanes and ships, because private businessmen were unable or unwilling to find the money. Businessmen have turned to the Government for protection against external and internal competition, and for subsidies in time of need. The Government, in turn, has intervened in the decisions of private businessmen whenever the public interest seemed to require it. While American history shows a strong preference for limited government, it also shows a strong desire to limit the power of private businessmen.

The functions of government vary according to the needs of the time. The assumption of new duties is sometimes supported by business, sometimes opposed. When President Kennedy denounced the attempted price increase by United States Steel Corporation in April 1962, most businessmen held up their hands in horror; but in 1911 Judge Elbert Gary, president of U.S. Steel, voluntarily suggested to Congress that steel prices should be regulated by the Federal Government. Most American businessmen see little inconsistency in appealing for Government assistance on one subject, while denouncing Government interference on another.

The attitudes of Americans towards the central government has, of course, been affected by the vastness of the country, which makes Washington sometimes appear in the guise of a foreign despot, and by the Jeffersonian tradition of self-reliant individualism. But this has not prevented the assumption of new powers by the Federal Government, usually in response to crises which could not be dealt with in any other way. In the past thirty years the Federal Government's responsibility to promote economic development has become wider and more explicit. The crisis that started this process was the Depression of the 1930s, which led to the 'New Deal' of President Franklin D. Roosevelt. Many of President Roosevelt's reforms had the effect of limiting the power of private businessmen – by encouraging the growth of labour unions, for example, by extending Government supervision over the stock exchanges, by creating Government-owned power systems to compete with the private electric utilities. The New Deal is sometimes said to have shifted the major sources of economic power from private to public institutions.

It was an unnerving experience for American businessmen, especially those who were directly affected by the reforms. Since then, the instinctive reaction of many businessmen to any proposed enlargement of Government authority has been vehement opposition. Fearful of further measures which might impose new constraints on management, they have tried to propagate the idea that America's economic progress has depended entirely on the effort and enterprise of individual businessmen.[3] They have played on the deep-rooted American belief in the 'inherent malevolence'[4] of government.

Despite this opposition, the legislation of the New Deal has for the most part remained intact. The responsibility of the Federal Government to 'promote maximum employment, production and purchasing power' was formally recognized in the Employment Act of 1946. It is possible that the anti-Government propaganda of the business community may have discouraged the Federal Government from any further innovations along the lines of the New Deal; this had been a period of radical reform which saw the establishment of institutions like the Tennessee Valley Authority, an experiment in Government-sponsored regional development which was widely admired overseas but which was attacked by businessmen at home as an example of 'creeping Socialism'.

In the postwar period there was no economic crisis to make radical reforms seem necessary. In the late 1950s, however, there was mounting dissatisfaction with the sluggish performance of the American economy, especially in contrast to the countries of Western Europe and Japan. After eight years of a Republican, business-oriented administration, President Kennedy took office in 1961 with a mandate to 'get America moving again'. Under President Kennedy and his successor, President Johnson, the Federal Government showed a greater willingness to innovate in the field of economic policy and to intervene in the decisions of businessmen than it had done in the preceding fifteen years.

Although some of the Administration's proposals have been opposed by businessmen, the last few years have also seen the emergence of a more rational, less dogmatic attitude on the part of the business community towards the Government's involvement with the economy. While the ideological controversies of the 1930s have not entirely faded away, there is a greater willingness to recognize that the United States now has – and to some extent always has had – a 'dual' or 'mixed' economy, in which government and business bear a joint responsibility for economic progress. The relationship between government and business is fluid. There will always be debate over such questions as how to reconcile the advantages of competition with the need for Government supervision in steel, electricity supply, and other key industries. But it seems that these questions are being tackled in a more pragmatic spirit than in the past. It is beginning to be recognized once again that innovations on the part of the Federal Government can make as useful a contribution to economic progress as innovation by businessmen.

2 · The Pressure of Competition

Seeking the Customer

MOST companies in most industries face a real possibility of losing part or all of their business if their customers can obtain better or cheaper service from rival concerns. They can react to this threat either offensively, by trying to stay ahead of their rivals, or defensively, by combining or conspiring with their rivals to eliminate competition. The principal objective of the antitrust laws, only partially fulfilled, is to ensure that the reaction is offensive.

Although the U.S. has a tradition and an institutional structure which encourages competition, it has not proved easy to preserve. Most businessmen want security for themselves and for their companies; competition involves insecurity. Not only are the antitrust laws often violated, but special exemptions for particular industries are frequently sought and sometimes granted. During the New Deal an attempt was made to suspend the antitrust laws and to replace competition with legalized cooperation, through the National Recovery Administration which lasted from 1933 to 1935. The experiment proved unworkable even before it was declared unconstitutional by the Supreme Court, but it was an indication of an ambivalent attitude towards competition on the part of both business and Government.

The Government can create competition, as it did for the electric utilities when it established the Tennessee Valley Authority in 1933, and again in 1946 when it transformed the structure of the aluminium industry. In the latter case the Government was faced after the war with the problem of selling to private industry the aluminium plants which had been built by the Government for war purposes. Before the war the only integrated producer of aluminium in the United States had been the Aluminium Company of America (Alcoa). This company had operated the state-owned plants during the war and was willing to purchase them from the Government. But despite difficulties caused by Alcoa's patent rights and its control of raw materials, the Government negotiated the sale of the plants to two other companies, with the result that, by 1948, Alcoa's share of the industry had been reduced to fifty per cent, with Reynolds accounting for about thirty per cent and Kaiser the remaining twenty per cent. Several other newcomers subsequently entered the industry.

Other aspects of the Government's postwar disposal programme, however, were strongly criticized for contributing to monopoly. In steel, for example, the Geneva plant in Utah, the largest steelworks built by the Government during the war, was sold to the largest company in the industry, United States Steel Corporation, even though several smaller companies were apparently eager to buy it. As one critic described the transaction, 'the agents of the government and servants of the people approved this bargain counter sale to the overlord of the American steel industry'.[1]

Whether for political or economic reasons, the Government has been willing to protect particular industries from the rigours of internal or external competition. These industries are often characterized by a large number of small firms, whose political weight is sometimes greater than that of the giant companies. In rather the same way, the Kennedy Administration's commitment to freer trade did not prevent bargains being struck with certain groups – the carpet makers, the glass manufacturers, the oil producers – which had vigorously pleaded for protection against foreign competition.

Over a wide area of the American economy, nevertheless, competition is a potent force for efficiency and progressiveness in industry. While it is possible to obtain protection through political action, the consensus of opinion is that competition must be maintained except where there is a strong social or economic case against it. In some industries, admittedly, ungentlemanly devices like price-cutting are frowned upon and common policies which fall short of antitrust violations serve to keep competition within bounds. But these arrangements are frequently upset by an enterprising newcomer or by an aggressive customer who demands better treatment. If a canner is dissatisfied with his tin-can supplies, he can make his own tin cans. If a tin-can maker is dissatisfied with his tinplate supplies, he can make his own tinplate. The necessity to compete is often unwelcome, but it exists; it creates a feeling of insecurity which discourages complacency and stimulates innovation.

This feeling of insecurity has been intensified by the changes that have taken place within the American economy over the past decade (1955–65). The first decade after the Second World War was marked by an extraordinarily high level of consumer demand, especially for durable products like cars and refrigerators. The demand had been built up during fifteen years of virtual stagnation as a result of the Depression and the War. As soon as American industry made the adjustment to peacetime conditions, it found itself in a prolonged sellers' market in which sales were limited only by the capacity to produce. But by about 1955 the great surge in demand was beginning to slow down. Tougher competition made it harder to raise prices. Supply caught up with demand, and manufacturers who had invested ambitiously in new plant and equipment found themselves with spare capacity on their hands.[2]

To maintain their sales and their profits, manufacturers were forced to cut costs and to search for new markets. Since the growth of demand was no longer automatic, they had to find ways of stimulating it. The need to innovate was urgent, but because almost all producers were under the same pressure, it was increasingly difficult to hit upon an innovation which was not soon matched by a rival company. Not only has research become even more important to a company that wishes to stay ahead in the competitive struggle, but the time required to bring new technical developments into commercial use has had to be shortened. When Du Pont, the world's largest chemical company, developed nylon during the war, it had fifteen years of monopoly profits to look forward to, but when it introduced Delrin, a high-strength plastic capable of replacing metal in some applications, in 1960, hardly a year elapsed before a rival product – Celcon, made by Celanese Corporation – was on the market. Similarly, several firms are working to produce rivals for Du Pont's Corfam, a new porous material designed to replace leather in shoes. In many industries prices were cut, profit margins were squeezed, and the initiative passed from seller to buyer.

Adding to the general feeling of insecurity was the reappearance in world markets, and especially in the American market, of countries whose industries had been severely damaged during the war. Helped by lower wages and, in some cases, more modern plant, European and Japanese companies began to sell aggressively in the U.S. and in other countries where American firms had been the dominant suppliers. In a few years the U.S. was transformed from a net exporter to a net importer of steel and cars. Import competition was especially severe in finished goods; their share in America's total import bill has doubled since the early 1950s. Even the most powerful firms were not immune; for example, the king of the razor blade market, Gillette, found its position threatened by the stainless steel blades imported by a small British company, Wilkinson Sword.

The invasion of small imported cars, which in 1959 accounted for ten per cent of the U.S. market, forced the car makers in Detroit to halt the trend towards more luxurious models and adopt a new approach to customer requirements. While the introduction of the 'compacts' succeeded in stemming the flood of imports, foreign cars remained popular enough to be a significant competitive factor – particularly important in an industry where three giant companies, General Motors, Ford, and Chrysler, tended to imitate each other instead of striking out in new directions. One company, Ford, was on the point of introducing a domestically-built rival to the Volkswagen, but (perhaps remembering its disastrous experience with a medium-priced car, the Edsel, in 1957) drew back at the last moment, relying on imports from its German and British subsidiaries to retain a share of the Volkswagen-sized market.

In some industries the invasion of foreign goods was resisted with demands for higher tariffs or import quotas; but even where the demands were partially satisfied, as in the case of textiles, foreign competition often remained strong enough to stimulate change and encourage modernization in the industry. The bicycle makers, for example, who had suffered severely from import competition in the early 1950s, persuaded the Government to raise the tariff, but at the same time they energetically developed new models and new marketing techniques, often borrowing ideas from their overseas rivals. By installing new machinery and reducing their labour costs, they brought prices down to a level that could match those of the foreign producers.

One of the important consequences of these developments has been a reorientation, on the part of a large section of American industry, towards the customer. Instead of producing goods in the knowledge that there would always be customers waiting to buy them, manufacturers have had to find the customer first, establish his requirements, and plan their production accordingly. Instead of confining themselves to their traditional product lines, they have had to take a broader view of their functions, re-examine their skills and capacities, and redeploy their resources to attack new markets. An oil company (Gulf) acquires a stake in the coal industry, and a coal producer (Consolidation Coal) makes a bid for an oil company, because they regard themselves as 'suppliers of energy'. As a Gulf official put it, 'any energy customer who finds it more economical to buy coal rather than oil or gas, is a customer lost to Gulf unless Gulf has coal to sell'. Under the slogan 'everything to wear', Genesco becomes an importer, manufacturer, and retailer of shoes and apparel. As 'managers of money in the food business', Consolidated Foods engages in manufacturing, wholesaling, and retailing.

Diversification at home and abroad, backward integration into raw-material production, forward integration towards the consumer, mergers and acquisitions – all these have been responses by American industry to new competitive challenges. Traditional attitudes towards marketing, towards relations with supplier and with customer, have been altered. Distinctions between markets and between industries have become blurred.

The metal producers, for example, are battling among themselves and with plastics, wood, paper, glass and textiles for markets which once 'belonged' to a single supplying industry. 'Start with the consumer and work back from there' is the principle which many companies are following. To a large extent the properties of the final product are not determined by the range of materials that is available, but rather the desired properties are established first and the necessary materials are then developed to meet the specifications. The level of steel demand used to be thought of as essentially derived from the level of activity in the economy and particularly in the steel-using industries. Under the impact of rising competition from imports and from substitute materials, this attitude has been superseded by an aggressive search for new uses of steel. The marketing men are taking over from the production men; new products (like extra-thin tinplate for cans) and more flexible pricing policies reflect the change of approach. Hard selling is backed by a detailed study of what the steel user will need in five or ten years' time. Like the aluminium companies, some steel firms made investments in property-development projects, so as to promote the use of steel in construction. (In the same way General Electric recently took control of an urban renewal programme in San Francisco, partly because the investment seemed attractive in itself, partly to promote the sale of G.E. appliances and to create a showcase for 'all-electric living'.)

Some of the same changes are taking place in the copper industry, where production has traditionally taken precedence over marketing. Seeing themselves as suppliers of materials rather than as copper producers, they look for new ways to satisfy their customers' requirements – sometimes diversifying into different industries (as Anaconda moved into aluminium), and sometimes cooperating with producers of other materials to develop new uses.

In the field of materials no market is secure. The paper industry tries to replace metal dustbins with paper containers. Polythene milk bottles are devised to replace paper cartons which had previously replaced glass bottles. The glass industry challenges synthetic fibres in the tyre-cord market and promotes fibre-glass as a substitute for steel in cars. Textile producers diversify into paper and plastics. The aluminium producers move towards the customer (making aluminium cans for the canning industry, for example), and the aluminium fabricators move backwards into basic aluminium production. The two big canning companies, Continental Can and American Can, aim to cover the whole packaging field, with interests in steel, aluminium, glass, plastics and paper. After building their reputations as manufacturers of tin cans, they were forced to move with the market and satisfy their consumers' packaging wants in a wider way. Determined to win a stake in the manufacture of cups, for example, American Can was open-minded in its choice of materials: 'We'll make cups from lichee nuts if that's profitable', said an official.

It was the aluminium industry, unencumbered by tradition and oriented, because of the newness of the product, towards marketing, which forced a new approach on the steel and copper producers. This is an example of the kind of invasion of one industry by another which has been an important source of innovation in apparently backward industries. The invasion of the machine-tool industry by the electronics companies and of the textile industry by the chemical producers infused new techniques, and new technologies, into industries whose own record of innovation had been meagre. The invader almost always has something to teach; the steel producers, which had left most of the research on metals to their customers, could learn from the plastics producers, whose research into materials enabled them to take the initiative in suggesting the displacement of steel in their customers' products.

The process of invasion often brings clashes between giants who previously had little contact with each other. General Foods, the country's largest food processor, had ousted Nestles to win a dominant position in the coffee market for its Maxwell House brand. It is now being challenged on two fronts by Procter & Gamble, the detergent producer, and Coca-Cola, the soft-drink company; both companies, with their strength in consumer marketing rather than in particular consumer products, had been led to acquire a stake in coffee as part of their diversification into food. Such moves sometimes inject new ideas into an industry. When Coca-Cola acquired Minute Maid, a frozen-orange-juice producer, in 1960, it was said to herald a switch 'from the business of selling orange juice as a breakfast medicine to the business of selling oranges in any and every form the public will take them'. Even companies with an apparently unassailable position in a particular market, like Eastman Kodak in amateur film, could not feel completely secure. Du Pont announced plans to introduce a rival product in association with Bell & Howell; although the project was eventually dropped, the knowledge of Du Pont's interest in the film market was a spur to Kodak's efforts to develop new products and new technologies. The potential entry of outsiders can be a powerful competitive factor even in seemingly monopolistic industries.

It was significant that Du Pont was prepared to make a direct assault on consumer markets from which it had previously steered clear. 'Where we can make an important technical accomplishment', said the president of the company, 'we must be prepared to carry our development closer and closer to the ultimate consumer.' Instead of selling Delrin, the new high-strength plastic material, to fabricators, Du Pont decided to make Delrin pipe and sell it direct to the oil industry and other users. (Electric tooth-brushes were recently added to Du Pont's line of consumer products.) Similarly, Union Carbide, once described as 'chemist to the chemical industry and metallurgist to the metal industry', decided that the best way to promote the use of urethane foam in mattresses was to acquire a mattress maker and participate in the business directly. Instead of passing on its technology for other people to use, the new policy is to retain it and make full use of it for the company's own purposes. This process of forward integration in the chemical industry reflects the policy, common to many industries, of finding particular needs 'in the marketplace' and tailoring products to meet them.

Most companies have resources of raw materials, plant and equipment, personnel, 'know-how', and cash which have been traditionally deployed in certain well-established directions, but which may be capable of being applied to other problems. The pressure of competition forces them to make the fullest possible use of their resources. A producer of oil and natural gas, for example, is no longer content to sell products to a textile company for conversion into nylon; it wants to participate, and hence it acquires the textile company. For some companies, notably in the electrical and chemical industries, the most important resource is not a particular commodity, like steel or oil, but their scientific excellence, their experience and ability in research and development, which, if given a free hand, will carry them far beyond their own industries. General Electric, which was originally concerned with electric power and with products that use electricity (like lamps), uses its technology to develop nuclear reactors and electronic computers; its watchword is not electricity, but 'the effective management of technology'. Similarly, Litton Industries, one of the fastest-growing electronics companies, develops 'technology' in its own laboratories and looks for commercial outlets for it; at the same time, it looks for technology in other companies that has not been commercially exploited, and tries to find applications for it.

It does not, of course, follow that only those companies which have a diversified spread of interests are likely to prosper. The most formidable competitors are often the companies which specialize in particular fields, like Caterpillar in earth-moving equipment or Timken in roller bearings. By concentrating his efforts in a limited market, the specialist can often be the largest-volume and lowest-cost producer and the leader in technological advance. As long as they stay ahead of their customers' requirements, companies can profit from 'sticking to their last'.

Equally, there is no automatic connexion between size of company and efficiency. In the steel industry the liveliest firms have often been the medium-sized producers, such as Inland, which has only one major steelworks in the Chicago area. (Even Inland, the sixth largest producer, is larger than any British steel company.) The giant United States Steel Corporation, which has a large number of plants throughout the country – its capacity is greater than that of the entire British steel industry – has found it difficult to coordinate them; the company has generally lagged in the application of new processes. It was described by one critic as 'a big, sprawling, inert giant, neither big because it was efficient nor efficient because it was big'.[3] In the last few years the company has been reorganized and streamlined, but its record shows that a wide spread of activities does not always confer advantages.

But it may happen that the specialist companies, being success-ful, generate cash more rapidly than can be readily absorbed in their traditional line of business. The chairman of Singer, the sewing-machine firm, describes the result:

> Successful companies in reasonably stable businesses [he says] tend to generate funds in excess of those required to support existing opera-tions. The Singer company found itself five years ago with assets of over $480m., supporting sales of $440m., and yielding an [after tax] profit of only $12m. In such circumstances companies must either diversify on a major scale or reduce excess assets to cash and return the cash to its owners.[4]

Champion Spark Plug is another example of a specialist which was forced to diversify in order to find an outlet for surplus cash. Managers of firms in this situation prefer using the cash to enlarge their own organizations to distributing it in higher dividends or higher wages.

Similarly, when a company's traditional business shows in-sufficient growth prospects, the managers are inclined to switch their effort and resources into something new. In theory, they should return the surplus cash to shareholders for them to re-invest as they think fit. In practice, most managers want their own organizations to grow and they do their own re-investing. Thus W. R. Grace, which had been basically a shipping and merchant-ing company, considered three possible areas of investment – chemicals, petroleum, and electronics. Once the decision had been made in favour of chemicals, resources were poured into it, so that in a few years' time the new field represented sixty to seventy per cent of the company's business.

This sort of process may have the undesirable effect of freezing the distribution of assets in the hands of existing companies. Many diversification ventures, moreover, have been unsuccessful. It could be argued that when Ford acquired Philco, a maker of domestic appliances and electronic equipment, it was supplying managerial acumen as well as cash to an ailing company, but there was no other link between them. (It was a 'conglomerate' merger, involving companies in distinct industries, as opposed to a 'horizontal' merger, involving companies that make a similar product, or a 'vertical' merger, involving companies related as supplier and customer.) As it turned out, Philco's problems were rather more difficult to solve than had been expected, and the rescue operation proved a heavy drain on Ford's resources. On the other hand, some conglomerate companies have had an impressive record of successful management. By branching out in all directions, they have contributed to the process of invasion which has been a fruitful source of progress in many industries.

Changes in Retailing

A similar process of change, and a similar blurring of traditional industry definitions, has been taking place in retailing. As in other countries, the distribution of goods from manufacturer to consumer had been one of the least efficient sectors of the American economy, but as long as consumer demand was insatiable and the market could always absorb price increases, the pressure to reduce costs was slight. But when demand began to slacken and competition to intensify, retailers found themselves facing the same problems as manufacturers. Traditional ways of doing business had to be altered.

The steady rise in retail prices had been largely due to the spiralling costs of retail and clerical labour. Hence an opportunity was available for someone who could economize on the use of labour – the discounter. 'The reorientation of retailing from the convenience of the merchant to the convenience of the consumer is due entirely to the explosive growth of discounting'. This claim, made by the head of a large discount group, may be exaggerated, but there is no doubt that the discounter, offering low prices based on a high rate of turnover and a minimum of customer services, has had a profound impact on conventional department stores. One discounter's operating expenses were said to run about forty per cent less than in a conventional department store, principally because of self-service, the elimination of unnecessary fixtures, and reliance on simple, single-storey structures.

The department stores were slow to respond to the challenge, partly because they had been enjoying a virtual monopoly. They had grown up in the second half of the nineteenth century in response to the development of the new urban market; the novel technique of offering a large variety of goods under one roof represented as big a threat to established retailing patterns as did the discount store a hundred years later. The key to the department store's prosperity was the city centre, or, as the Americans call it, downtown. As Professor McNair has said:

So long as downtown remained supreme and the customers for the wide range of department store merchandise had no alternative but to come downtown, the traditional department store was almost invulnerable. Sheltered behind its monolithic downtown fortress, with highly limited possible locations, it enjoyed a species of monopoly.[5]

But the spectacular growth of the suburbs during the postwar years undermined the basis of the department store's supremacy and created an opportunity which the discount stores were quick to fill.

The department store companies were forced to reappraise their attitudes to store location (many of them had been traditionally single-store institutions), to prices and margins, and to services. In many cases the 'service' provided by their shop assistants was almost non-existent; they had to choose between eliminating it, and thus matching the discounter's prices, or improving it to the point where it became a significant competitive advantage.

Discounting, once described as nothing more than selling inferior goods on a Sunday, soon became an established part of the retailing scene. By 1963 the discounters were claiming nine per cent of the nation's retail sales, compared with thirteen per cent for the department stores and thirty-nine per cent for food supermarkets. Like most new and fast-growing industries, it went through a period of 'shake-out' which involved a number of bankruptcies. In some cases the quality of management was found to be inadequate as the size of the business grew. Even E. J. Korvette, the pioneer of the discount movement, ran into financial difficulties, partly because of an unfortunate venture into food, partly, perhaps, because of the hazards of 'trading up'. The company preferred to describe itself as a 'promotional department store', and made a bid for respectability by opening a handsome branch in Fifth Avenue, New York, one of the most elegant and expensive shopping streets in the world.

A small number of powerful companies is likely to emerge out of the crowd of companies which have jumped on to the discounters' bandwagon; the survival of a few giants seems assured. At the same time, the entry into discounting of old-established retailers like Woolworth and S. S. Kresge, both heavily engaged in the relatively stagnant field of variety stores, suggests that the discount movement is not about to disappear. As the department stores fight back, sometimes with the discounters' own weapons, the line between them is blurred, but the search for new methods of cutting costs and improving service continues.

Quite apart from the rise of the discounter, there is intense competition in other sectors of retailing, with pressure on margins stimulating new ways of cutting costs and improving service. The supermarket industry, having expanded more rapidly than was justified by the demand, was forced to reappraise its pricing policy and, in cooperation with the food manufacturers, to increase efficiency in distribution. Some companies added non-food interests, and even branched out into discounting. Others took steps to reduce their purchasing costs by investing in their own manufacturing plants; Safeway, one of the biggest supermarket groups, which now operates several stores in Britain, owns or leases over 130 plants which manufacture products accounting for thirty per cent of its sales.

The need for more cooperation between manufacturer and retailer was increasingly recognized, especially in the supermarket field. As a study by McKinsey,[6] the management consultants, put it:

Both manufacturers and food chains are finding it increasingly difficult to improve profits. The chains can no longer rely, to nearly the degree that they did in the past, on new stores, mergers, or price increases to build profits. At the same time, manufacturers are finding it much more difficult now than in the 1950's to launch successful new products, raise prices, or consummate mergers.

Hence cooperation was essential to extract greater yield from existing stores and existing product lines. General Foods subsequently commissioned McKinsey to make an intensive study of the economics of food distributors.[7] It was realized that the rate of growth of food sales was slowing down, that the industry was 'overstored', that wages in retailing were rising much more rapidly than productivity, and that profits were declining. Hence a variety of possible areas for cost reduction were examined – store location, store size, pricing, control of labour, choice of products; the last of these was particularly appropriate for retailer–manufacturer cooperation, since it was possible to identify precisely the costs and profits associated with a particular product line, and to recommend action, by manufacturer or retailer, to reduce costs – a different size of case, different opening devices, different methods of transportation and so on.

Major sales advantages [concludes the report] can accrue to the progressive suppliers – that is, the ones who learn more about the distributor's profitability on their products and then act on this knowledge to reshape their promotions, packaging, merchandising methods, and even sales organizations.

The manufacturers, for their part, joined in the general process of experimentation. Some moved directly into retailing, without losing their ties to existing retailers; this practice of 'dual distribution', much criticized by some retailers, was followed especially by makers of soft goods, like shoes and apparel. Botany Industries, a large clothing manufacturer, regarded its seventy-five retail outlets as 'laboratories' in which it could study trends in styling and design. In the field of domestic appliances, Westinghouse opened an experimental retail store of its own, and its rival, General Electric, introduced a 'sales and display' franchise, whereby a franchised dealer, with a full line of G.E. appliances, would be freed of the responsibility for stocking and deliveries; this would be carried out from a nearby G.E. distributing centre. Thus the dealer, carrying no stocks and spared the task of collecting appliances from the G.E. warehouse and delivering them to customers, is able to concentrate on sales and promotion.

These moves by manufacturers aroused fears that the independent retailer would be squeezed out of existence; but in other sectors the small, independent retailers were showing remarkable vitality, banding together in voluntary groups to gain the advantages, in mass buying power, of the big chains, without losing the flexibility that derives from independent ownership. There was some evidence that the small retailer was staging a come-back against the giants. As the consumer market became more diverse and sophisticated, there was scope for specialized attention to particular consumer needs. The big chains, with their stress on mass-volume selling and low prices, left gaps in the market which the small retailer was often able to fill.

All these developments reflected the fluidity of retailing. Competition came from unexpected sources. (There was even a suggestion that the American Farm Bureau Federation, the principal farmers' organization, might purchase the Great Atlantic and Pacific Tea Company, the nation's largest supermarket chain, to give farmers a direct stake in the distribution of their products.) Some experiments failed; others seemed likely to lead to far-reaching changes in traditional patterns. Retailers, like manufacturers, began to study consumer needs more closely and adopt new ways of satisfying them. One obvious way was to take advantage of the shift in consumer spending from goods to services. Sears Roebuck, the nation's largest and most successful merchandiser, already operated an insurance company and now planned to start its own mutual fund. Federated Department Stores, one of the liveliest department store groups, was examining new opportunities in the restaurant business, in the travel field, in home maintenance, in prepared foods, dry cleaning, shoe repairs, and other fields. The growing tendency for people to hire, and not to own, cars, appliances and other goods, pointed to new ways in which the retailer could serve the public.

Impact on Management

The intensity of competition throughout the American economy is probably responsible for one of the major differences between American and European businessmen; the Americans pay a much more minute attention to cost reduction and profit improvement.

But the growth of trade between Europe and the United States, and the presence of many American-owned companies in Europe, ensures that new ideas are quickly transmitted across the Atlantic. The gradual development of a tariff-free European market, together with Government policies to stimulate competition, should also help to encourage in Europe more of an American-style attitude towards marketing.

Competitive conditions do not, of course, ensure that an industry's performance will be adequate. Competition is simply one way of bringing pressure on businessmen to reduce their costs and improve their products. Although there are signs of a reorientation towards the customer on the part of American industry, this does not mean that the customer is sovereign. Any business enterprise is primarily concerned with its own profitability and success; the relationship between profits and the public interest is not automatic. The operations of private companies may involve social costs which call for intervention from the Government. For example, the growth of car ownership has created problems of safety on the roads and pollution of the atmosphere. Special Government measures are necessary to force the manufacturers to pay more attention to these problems in the design of their vehicles. The need for special precautions to protect the interests of the consumer is reflected in such institutions as the Food and Drug Administration, whose task is to guard against adulteration and misbranding, and the Federal Trade Commission, part of whose function is to guard against false or misleading advertisements.

The Government needs a variety of weapons to influence and control the behaviour of businessmen. One of the most important weapons, nevertheless, must be the power to stimulate competition. The antitrust laws have helped to shape the competitive environment in which American businessmen operate. As competition intensifies, moreover, so businessmen are inclined to find new ways of evading it. Far from declining in importance in the post-1955 period, the antitrust laws have recently been strengthened; their importance as a constraint on management is probably greater now than it has ever been in the past.

35

3 · Antitrust and Market Power

The Control of Business

THE sharpening of competition during the past decade has improved the performance of American industry. But it has not relieved the central government of the need to scrutinize, interfere with, and sometimes control the behaviour of businessmen. Most businessmen are chiefly concerned with the health and profitability of their own enterprises. The government is concerned with the community as a whole, and with the interests of consumers in particular.

It was to protect the interests of consumers in the late nineteenth century that the Government imposed two new constraints on businessmen. The predatory practices of giant companies, including the railways, John D. Rockefeller's Standard Oil Company, and the sugar trust ('gluttons of luxury and power', as they were called), and the alarming trend towards mergers, cartels and concentration, aroused fierce resentment among consumers, especially the farmers; their demands for reform forced the state governments and then the Federal Government to take action. In effect, businessmen were told that they must either compete, fairly and openly, with one another, or, if competition was unworkable, they must accept some form of Government supervision. These two approaches, enforced by the antitrust laws on the one hand and by Government regulation on the other, have remained the principal elements in public policy towards industry.

Neither approach has been wholly successful. The antitrust laws have been neglected for most of their history, and Government regulation has often seemed to hamper progress in the regulated industries. Of the two, antitrust seemed to accord better with the nation's traditional faith in competition and the dispersal of power, but it proved more difficult to enforce – largely because of business hostility. Businessmen could influence in their own interests the Interstate Commerce Commission, created in 1886 to regulate the railways, and similar agencies created for other industries, but the effect of the antitrust laws was unpredictable and potentially dangerous. For over a decade the Sherman Act of 1890, the first of the antitrust laws, was virtually forgotten, and it failed to obstruct the nation's first great merger movement, which reached its peak in 1898–1902 and imposed on American industry the basic structure that has persisted to this day. It was during this period that such giants as American Tobacco and American Can, U.S. Rubber and U.S. Steel, International Paper and International Harvester, were formed.

The Sherman Act was rescued from oblivion by President Theodore Roosevelt and his successor, President Taft. In the Northern Securities case of 1904 J. P. Morgan, the chief promoter of mergers, was prevented by the Supreme Court from amalgamating two railway companies, and in 1911 the Court ordered the dissolution of American Tobacco and Standard Oil. But while these rulings showed that the Sherman Act had teeth, the Court interpreted the Act in a way which severely limited its application. Just as Roosevelt himself popularized the distinction between 'good' and 'bad' trusts, so a majority of justices on the Supreme Court insisted that 'mere size', or 'the existence of unexerted power', was not an offence; only if the power conferred by size was abused, the majority argued, was the Sherman Act transgressed. Under this so-called 'rule of reason', U.S. Steel, International Harvester and other 'trusts', escaped dismemberment, and the Sherman Act was increasingly directed, not against corporate consolidations, but against agreements among competitors to fix prices or allocate markets.

Pricing Policy

This is one of the few provisions in the antitrust laws which have been rigorously enforced. Though there were fears that, by preventing companies from cooperating, the Government was encouraging them to merge and thus promoting 'trustification', the general prohibition against price-fixing, and the severe penalties and moral opprobrium which convicted offenders incur, have kept the American economy remarkably free of those gentlemen's agreements among competitors which have been common in European industry. Businessmen sometimes complain that, through fear of seeming to 'conspire' with their competitors, they are inhibited from exchanging technical information, or agreeing on common standards which would assist the industry's customers. But despite these difficulties the bias against 'conspiracy' is deeply ingrained in the American business system, and, to this extent, the antitrust laws have succeeded in stimulating competition.

Prices must not be 'fixed', but it does not follow that only prices which respond immediately to changes in supply and demand accord with the antitrust laws. There is nothing illegal about price stability.

What we want from competition [one economist has observed] is a process by means of which over the long run, and not too long a run at that, consumers get the results of a vigorous and independent probing of the possibilities of cost and price reductions in the American economy by independent buyers and sellers.[1]

This process certainly does not imply that prices should be volatile.

Extreme instability in prices is usually harmful for an industry and for the economy as a whole, and the Federal Government has sometimes tried to eliminate 'ruinous' price competition in certain industries (such as coal) even at the expense of granting them an exemption from the antitrust laws. In a large part of agriculture, for example, competition has been lessened or eliminated. By guaranteeing to buy farm products at a certain price, the Government runs the risk of encouraging overproduction, but a reasonably stable industry, free from sudden price and income fluctuations, is likely to be more efficient, more willing to innovate and invest in new processes. When price supports were introduced for potatoes in the Second World War, it led to much greater specialization in potato production, a faster adoption of new technology, a rapid rise in yield per acre and a reduction in prices.[2] Violent fluctuations in copper prices, reflecting swings in supply and demand, have encouraged copper users to switch to alternative materials, like aluminium, where the price movements were more predictable.

In other cases price stability may be impossible to achieve without offending against the antitrust laws. The circumstances that led to the great electrical conspiracy, in which twenty-nine manufacturers, including General Electric and Westinghouse, were convicted of price-fixing and seven senior executives sent to prison, were the severe cyclical fluctuations in demand. Orders from the electric utilities came in large units at irregular intervals, and in the intervening periods the suppliers were sorely tempted to cut prices drastically to get new business. These price wars were so disastrous that the conspiracy was started in order to keep prices (and profits) stable. The antitrust conviction in 1960 brought the conspiracy to an end (and provided ample material for sermons on the morals of businessmen), but the genuine problem of achieving a more stable relationship between electrical equipment suppliers and the utilities was left unsolved.

In industries where there are few sellers, the phenomenon of 'price leadership' is common. This is not illegal and not necessarily undesirable. But it suggests the possibility that competitive forces are not as strong as they should be, especially if profits in the industry appear to be high in relation to other industries. The antitrust laws are only relevant if there is actual collusion among the sellers. In the tobacco case of 1946 the Supreme Court ruled that there was a price conspiracy among the cigarette producers, though some observers thought the ruling simply extended the meaning of the word 'conspiracy'. The effect of the ruling was to encourage a more restrained pricing policy on the part of the industry, but it did not do much to increase competition.

Similar problems arise in the case of steel. That there is a public interest in the pricing of steel, because of its importance to the economy, no one denies, and it is sometimes urged that American steel prices should be publicly regulated, as they are in Britain by the Iron and Steel Board. The traditional price leader, U.S. Steel, is said to have followed a pricing policy coloured by a concept of itself as the industry leader 'vested with the responsibilities and subject to the inhibitions of a public utility'.[3] Because U.S. Steel has not been the lowest-cost producer, its role as the price leader may have kept prices higher than they need have been. This is one of several reasons why some observers believe that the Supreme Court's decision not to break up U.S. Steel in 1920 was bad for the industry.

The antitrust laws have frequently been invoked in an attempt to change the steel industry's pricing practices – in the 1920s when the 'Pittsburgh plus' system was prohibited and again in the 1940s when the multiple basing point system was abolished. These decisions were intended to increase the flexibility of steel prices. More recently the stature of U.S. Steel as the price leader has been weakened as its share of the industry's output declined. In the three years following President Kennedy's clash with the industry, a series of antitrust suits has been filed. In one of these eight leading companies were fined $50,000 each, the maximum permitted under the Sherman Act, for allegedly conspiring to fix the price of 'extras' on sheet steel. This case involved the mainly technical question of whether meetings to agree on a schedule of 'extras' to be charged for special qualities and sizes should be regarded as price-fixing or as a necessary service to the public. These suits were an embarrassment to the industry, but they may have contributed to an apparent increase in price competition during the last few years. Yet early in 1966 the head of the Antitrust Division of the Justice Department was still insisting that pricing in steel was 'essentially non-competitive'.

He was referring to the fact that in a concentrated industry like steel there is a sense in which the leading firms can 'set' or 'administer' their own prices, aiming for a certain rate of return on capital over a long period. This has meant that these industries have tended not to raise prices sharply when demand is booming (as often happens in more fragmented industries) and not to cut prices sharply when demand falls off. This may be unobjectionable, but it means that a considerable degree of pricing discretion is enjoyed by these large firms, and their pricing decisions may not accord with the Government's view of the public interest. It was argued, for example, that the 'market power' of the steel companies allowed them to raise prices sharply between 1955 and 1957, thus contributing both to inflation and to a drop in America's share of world steel exports.

There had been an earlier occasion, in 1949, when President Truman had warned the steel companies that, if they did not rapidly expand their production capacity, he would recommend that the Government should build its own steel mills. The steel industry in the United States, as in many other countries, has frequently been subjected to criticism and exhortation from the Government, because its performance is regarded as crucial to the economy as a whole. But it is its price behaviour which has been the centre of attention during the last few years. While the Antitrust Division of the Justice Department has been looking for evidence of price-fixing and collusion, both President Kennedy and President Johnson used every opportunity to remind the steelmakers of their responsibility to the nation; whenever there was talk in the trade of a possible rise in prices, a firm statement on the need for price stability would come from the President. In the summer of 1965 President Johnson's Council of Economic Advisers published a detailed report on the industry, showing how price increases of 1955–7 had contributed to the loss of export markets, and arguing that since 1962 productivity had been rising faster than employment costs, so that no price increase was justified. Later in the year the Council reacted angrily when Bethlehem Steel raised prices on structural steel by $5 a ton. But U.S. Steel, which had been the centre of the pricing storm in 1962, pleased the Administration by announcing a much smaller increase and coupling it with reductions on other steel products; Bethlehem soon followed suit. Similarly, an attempted price increase in aluminium was rescinded under pressure from President Johnson.

Whether this mixture of rigorous antitrust enforcement, price leadership within the industry, and exhortation from the Government will produce the right results remains to be seen. There is little doubt that the open discussion of the issues, which is supplemented by frequent examinations of the industry by Congressional committees, has had a restraining effect on prices. It has also contributed to a better understanding of the industry's position on the part of the general public. While some people insist that the government has no right to meddle in price decisions of private companies, there is considerable support for the view that large companies in some concentrated industries possess a substantial degree of market power and that the Government has a right to influence how that power is used.

Market Power

The same problem can be attacked at its root, by using the antitrust laws to reduce or eliminate the market power of large firms. This was, indeed, the original purpose of the Sherman Act, but the introduction of the 'rule of reason' limited the Act to situations where market power was abused. It was partly to correct this deficiency that the Clayton Act of 1914 was passed. Section 7 of the Act prohibited stock acquisitions by companies 'where the effect of such acquisition may be to substantially lessen competition or tend to create a monopoly'. But the effect of the Act was soon nullified. Instead of acquiring the stock of a competing firm, the acquiring company could purchase its entire assets; asset acquisitions were outside the Clayton Act's jurisdiction. Hence neither the Sherman Act nor the Clayton Act were able to prevent the nation's second merger movement, which reached its peak in 1926–30 and would have continued but for the Depression. During this period some industries were transformed from near-monopolies into oligopolies; in steel and chemicals, for example, Bethlehem Steel and Allied Chemical emerged as powerful rivals for the established giants, U.S. Steel and Du Pont. The effect of the mergers was to increase the concentration of assets in the hands of the largest firms, but in particular industries the degree of monopoly control was lessened. Other industries, however, where small firms had been dominant, were transformed by the creation of giants like General Foods in food processing, General Mills in flour milling, and National Dairy in milk distribution.

Surprisingly, it was only towards the end of the 1930s that the process of industrial concentration began to be considered as a possible explanation of the inadequate performance of the economy. It was at that time that the antitrust agencies – the Antitrust Division of the Justice Department and the Federal Trade Commission, which was created in 1914 – were given larger budgets and staff, and a full-scale investigation of the structure of industry was undertaken by the Temporary National Economic Committee. The exhaustive T.N.E.C. hearings failed to produce any convincing link between mergers and the Depression, but it gave a new impetus to antitrust legislation. In the Alcoa case of 1946 the view that, while price-fixing agreements were illegal *per se*, monopoly power was only illegal if it was abused was firmly rejected by Judge Hand. His ruling, calling for an end to Alcoa's monopoly of the aluminium industry, indicated a reversal of the 'rule of reason' and a revival of the Sherman Act as a weapon against mergers and market power.

It is the Supreme Court which is the final arbiter of the antitrust laws, and changes in the composition of the Court can lead to different interpretations of the laws. Two years after the Alcoa case, the Court moved a step backwards towards the 'rule of reason', when it permitted U.S. Steel to acquire Columbia Steel, a large independent steel fabricator on the west coast. In a five-to-four decision the majority admitted that a restriction on competition was involved in the merger, but argued that the restriction was not 'unreasonable'. Justice Douglas, speaking for the dissenting judges, insisted that the key issue was the existence of monopoly power.

It can be benign or it can be dangerous. The philosophy of the Sherman Act is that it should not exist. Power that controls the economy should be in the hands of elected representatives of the people, not in the hands of an industrial oligarchy. Industrial power should be decentralized. It should be scattered into many hands so that the fortunes of the people will not be dependent on the whim or caprice, the political prejudices, the emotional stability of a few self-appointed men.

The Columbia Steel decision came at a time when the third (and still continuing) merger movement was beginning to gather pace. Assuming that the Sherman Act was powerless to halt this movement, Congress decided to strengthen the Clayton Act and in 1950, through the Celler–Kefauver amendment, it was altered to cover asset as well as stock acquisitions. This was a valuable new weapon. A few years later the composition of the Supreme Court changed again, and the philosophy expressed by Justice Douglas in his Columbia Steel dissent began to prevail. Justice Douglas spoke for the majority in the Lexington Bank case of 1963, which prohibited a merger between two banks in Lexington, Kentucky; the ruling suggested that any merger between two firms that were significant factors in a particular market could be blocked almost as easily as a price-fixing agreement. This was a return to the principle of the Northern Securities case of 1904, before the 'rule of reason' had been applied to the Sherman Act. Finally, a special bonus for the trust-busters was the Supreme Court's revival of the pre-1950 Clayton Act (applying to stock acquisitions) when it ruled that the stockholding acquired by Du Pont in General Motors in 1919 was illegal and had to be sold. This was a special situation involving two of the very largest firms in the country, but the ruling opened up the possibility that a giant firm like General Motors itself, whose early growth had involved a number of mergers, could be attacked on the ground that the mergers, though unobjectionable at the time, had led to the creation of a monopolistic industry. The head of the Antitrust Division warned that the Du Pont–G.M. ruling provided 'the only available tool in selected cases to help restore to an over-concentrated industry the competitive vigor it has lost'.

Armed with these new weapons, the Government seemed to be in a strong position to arrest the merger movement and to prevent the concentration of industrial power into fewer hands. After 1950 there was a sharp increase in antitrust activity. Between 1951 and 1964 the Antitrust Division of the Justice Department and the Federal Trade Commission together challenged 143 mergers, nearly twice as many as in the preceding thirty-six years. Backed by a sympathetic Supreme Court, the authorities moved with particular severity against any giant firms which tried to expand by merger.

There was no doubt that the two earlier merger movements

had increased the importance in the economy of the hundred largest companies. Though the process was checked between 1930 and 1947, it was estimated that between 1947 and 1962 the share of the hundred largest manufacturing firms in the 'value added' by manufacturing industry as a whole rose from 23 per cent to 32 per cent. There was a tendency for the giant firms to become more nearly equal in size, but there was a marked decline in the frequency of change in the identities of the giant firms and in the frequency of change in relative size positions among the giants.[4]

As for mergers, more than 11,000 of them were recorded by the Federal Trade Commission between 1950 and 1964. Since 1950 the 200 largest industrial corporations acquired more than 2,000 other firms, and 257 of the 1,000 largest manufacturing corporations disappeared through merger during this period. Many of the mergers were 'conglomerate', involving the entry of a large company into a new field. Thus, while the over-all weight of the largest firms has increased, the degree of concentration within particular industries has shown no significant trend. Some oligopolies became more 'oligopolistic', but in others the number of sellers increased. There remained, nevertheless, a substantial number of highly concentrated industries in which a few firms wielded considerable market power.

There were reasonable grounds for concern about these trends. The wholesale fragmentation of large and successful firms was clearly impracticable; some degree of market power was the unavoidable consequence of size. But a legitimate objective of public policy was to keep this power within bounds, to prevent it from being enlarged, and to stimulate competition wherever possible. On social grounds, the dominance of a few large firms, with strong positions in a number of separate industries, was in direct conflict with the traditional American belief in the decentralization of power. As one justice had said:

It is possible, because of its indirect social or moral effect, to prefer a system of small producers, each dependent for his success on his own skill and character, to one in which the great mass of those engaged must accept the direction of the few.

The antitrust authorities began to move vigorously against any giant firm which tried to expand by merger. General Motors, for example, was attacked by the Justice Department for acquiring an earthmoving-equipment maker and a locomotive maker. When Chrysler proposed to buy Mack, one of the smaller commercial vehicle makers, the move was promptly challenged by the authorities and abandoned before the case reached the courts. When Standard Oil of New Jersey, the country's largest oil company, proposed to buy Tidewater's west-coast refining and marketing facilities, it was blocked by the Justice Department, even though it could be argued that the deal would increase competition for the dominant west-coast firm, Standard Oil of California. It became clear that, in the authorities' view, a large firm must expand 'from within', using its own resources to enter a new market or a new industry. The result of preventing the Bethlehem Steel–Youngstown merger, for example, was to oblige Bethlehem Steel to build its own integrated steelworks in the Chicago market instead of making use of Youngstown's existing facilities.

Preserving Small Business

A second, and more dubious, line of approach followed by the trust-busters was to prevent a fragmented industry from becoming less fragmented or from being invaded by a giant from outside. In the Brown Shoe–Kinney case of 1962 the Supreme Court was strongly influenced by the view that one of the purposes of the antitrust laws was 'to preserve, for its own sake and in spite of possible cost, an organization of industry in small units which can effectively compete with each other'. Even though the merger between two small shoe manufacturers might have produced a more efficient company, it might also, the Court feared, have started a process of concentration in the industry which would have eliminated many small producers.

If this policy was adopted on a large scale, it would prevent a 'rationalization' of industries whose existing structure is not conducive to efficiency. As yet, the authorities appear to be taking a pragmatic approach. They did not intervene, for example, in the textile industry where a series of mergers led to the emergence of a few large firms, like Burlington and J.P. Stevens, with a substantial share of the market. The consolidation process in this industry helped to bring stability into a market where, because of the large number of weak sellers, there had been chronic over-capacity and destructive price competition. Similarly, the emergence of large firms like Bobbie Brooks and Jonathan Logan in the garment manufacturing trade improved the industry's bargaining position with the textile companies on one side and the big chain stores on the other. In the road-haulage industry, too, there was no attempt to interfere with a merger process that was creating larger and stronger firms, able to invest in new machinery and new management techniques.

But the Brown Shoe decision reflected a solicitude for small business which has led both to exemptions from the antitrust laws for small businessmen and to the use of the laws to protect small businessmen. There is a certain nostalgia for the 'yeomanry' of small business, as if the character of small businessmen were somehow more estimable than that of big businessmen; the encouragement of small business is regarded as an essential counterweight to the power of the giant corporations. Small businessmen have been able to capitalize on this sentiment in order to win a measure of protection from the rigours of competition.

The Robinson-Patman Act of 1936 (an amendment to the Clayton Act) was a Depression-born measure designed to protect small retailers from the discriminatory lower prices which were secured by their large rivals, the chain stores, by virtue of their greater purchasing power. This price-discrimination law is generally agreed to be necessary, but it has proved difficult to administer. Its effect has been to make buyers more reluctant to press for price concessions, and sellers more chary of granting them, so that the flexibility of the price system has been reduced.[5] The law's attempt to control the price behaviour of firms had failed. As one critic has put it:

The Act proceeds on the general philosophy, reinforced with a number of specific but cloudy ground rules, calculated to require both buyers and sellers to hold an umbrella over less favoured competitors, always to the disadvantage of the ultimate consumer. We are permitted to meet but not beat a competitor's special price, a posture that makes no commercial sense. But before we can even meet the competitor's special price, we must determine that *his* price is a legal one for him, a question usually impossible to answer while the sale is being contested, and so on ad infinitum.[6]

A more obvious conflict with the antitrust states are the 'fair trade' or resale price maintenance laws which are in force in some states. Before the Depression, resale price maintenance was as illegal as any other form of price-fixing, but the Miller–Tydings Act of 1937 permitted the states to pass their own 'fair trade' laws, allowing manufacturers to fix the retail price of their products. Although the Federal antitrust authorities have consistently argued against these laws, they have not been declared unconstitutional by the Supreme Court; they were in fact strengthened in 1951, when the McGuire Act permitted manufacturers in fair trade states to enforce their prices even on 'non-signers', retailers who did not sign a formal agreement with their suppliers. About half the states have these laws, varying considerably in scope and effectiveness.

It has been estimated that consumers in states with fair trade laws pay prices that are higher, by amounts ranging from 19 per cent to 27 per cent, than prices in states without such laws.

This price disparity was used as an argument in the successful campaign to abolish resale price maintenance in the U.K. – a move which has already had a considerable impact on competition in retail trade. In the United States resale price maintenance is not yet dead; there have been many attempts to persuade Congress to enact a Federal fair trade statute, which would authorize resale price maintenance on a national level. But the laws have not prevented the discounters from winning a substantial share of the nation's retail business. Moreover, the Federal authorities are quick to take action against firms which withhold supplies from cut-price stores. There is some evidence that support for resale price maintenance is declining – many firms have found it virtually impossible to enforce even in fair trade states.

There are certainly sound social and economic reasons for ensuring that small businessmen have a fair competitive chance and are not swamped by the superior resources of the giants. But there are more constructive ways of assisting them than by insulating them from competition. The Small Business Administration, for example, created by the Federal Government in 1953 as a successor to the Reconstruction Finance Corporation, channels aid to small businessmen in the form of advice, training and loans. One of the most important of the S.B.A.'s programmes is the sponsorship of Small Business Investment Companies, in which private investors are encouraged by the promise of matching Government funds and favourable tax treatment of profits and losses to help in financing small businesses.[7] The Federal Government might also assist in financing the cooperative buying organizations which have enabled some retailer groups to compete effectively against the chain stores. What is needed is not protection from competition, but rather an improvement in the small businessman's techniques and resources, so that he is able to compete.

Antitrust policy needs to be flexible and non-doctrinaire, and its limitations have to be recognized. It is misleading to present the issue as a stark choice between 'the commissar system' and 'the autonomous forces of the marketplace', as did a recent chief of the Antitrust Division. It is important that large firms should be subject to competition, but unrealistic to suppose that market power can be eliminated. It has to be recognized that mergers often play a vital role as industries adapt to changing technologies and changing markets, and that the invasion of one industry by another is often a fruitful source of progress. The ability of small firms to sell out to large firms is essential to facilitate the mobility of resources.

When a very large firm proposes to expand by merger, it is reasonable to err on the side of toughness in interpreting and administering the antitrust laws. As one economist has put it:

The worst that a wrong merger decision can do is to force a company to build rather than buy. There will be cases where this means not building either, but they will be few and usually only a private loss to the concern which might have made a good buy.[8]

Although the trust-busters are sometimes accused of confusing the need to preserve competition with the need to preserve competitors, the existence of independent centres of initiative is normally essential to the health and progressiveness of an industry. In brewing, for instance, the authorities are aware of the economic factors leading towards mergers, but are determined to keep the process of concentration under control; if the industry ends up with ten large firms rather than five, the chances of vigorous competition will be very much greater.

A tough policy towards mergers, on the recent American pattern, may be less appropriate in countries like the U.K. where the size of firms is generally much smaller than in the U.S. The British Government has taken steps to strengthen the laws which promote competition; these are administered through the Monopolies Commission, which deals mainly with mergers, and the Restrictive Practices Court, which is concerned mainly with price-fixing. But it is also recognized that many industries are too fragmented, and that a greater degree of concentration, through mergers, would make for greater efficiency; as in the United States, the textile industry is going through this process, though in Britain's case the stimulus came from outside companies, such as Courtaulds and Imperial Chemical Industries, for which the textile industry was an important customer. Britain needs to encourage those mergers which lead to longer production runs and greater economies of scale. Public policy towards competition and concentration is still in a rudimentary state in Britain, but it is recognized that the greater fragmentation of industry, and the smaller size of the market, call for a somewhat different approach than has been adopted in the United States.

A Flexible Approach

Even in America, of course, there is nothing fixed about public policy towards mergers. There is a bias against mergers involving the very largest companies, but each case has to be examined on its merits. The issues in merger cases are often very complex. The economics of the industry may have to be examined in very great detail to determine whether or not the behaviour or proposed action of the firm can be considered 'monopolistic'. This may lead to a long delay, perhaps extending for several years, before the case is finally disposed of; the firms involved have to put up with a highly uncertain situation for a long period.

It is possible that some of this uncertainty could be eliminated. The Federal Trade Commission was originally created to take an administrative approach to the regulation of anti-competitive practices, although in practice it has tended to duplicate the work of the Justice Department (in addition to its other function of policing false advertising and commercial bribery). There have been suggestions that when there are signs of growing concentration in an industry, the F.T.C. should make a complete study of its structure, competitive conduct, cost and price performance, and other factors, with a view to promulgating rules that would define the permissible limit of horizontal and vertical mergers in the industry. This approach was used in 1965 on the dairy industry, where the largest companies, such as National Dairy and Borden, had made numerous acquisitions of smaller companies. The Commission recognized that there was a minimum economic size for dairy production, and that some of the acquired firms were below it, but it insisted that technological factors of this sort did not dictate the rise of vast, national, multi-plant companies. In a deliberate attempt to influence the structure of the industry, the Commission aimed to create a healthy 'middle tier' of medium-sized companies capable of competing effectively with the giants. It is not certain how far this approach can be extended, but it represents an attempt to take some of the vagueness out of antitrust enforcement. Similarly the Justice Department intends to produce a series of guidelines covering mergers and other areas of antitrust activity.

Some degree of vagueness is bound to remain, and such phrases as 'undue market power' will never be completely defined. It is probably wrong to look for the same sort of '*per se*' prohibition of mergers between large firms as there is in the case of price-fixing agreements. The performance of the industry has to be taken into account, and there is no one industry structure which guarantees effective performance. Similarly, a firm's ability to win a dominant share of a market does not necessarily involve monopolistic practices. 'Having been urged to compete,' one judge remarked, 'a firm must not be turned upon when it wins.'

The huge size of General Motors, with nearly 60 per cent of the car market, is embarrassing to the trust-busters, especially as the number of 'independent' manufacturers (apart from the other two giants, Chrysler and Ford) has dwindled steadily. With the demise of Studebaker in 1964, only American Motors was left, and this company, which had pioneered the 'compact' car as a rival for the low-priced imports, was now running into difficulties. It was apparently unable to find a niche in the market that was not already covered by General Motors, and its limited resources discouraged it from further pioneering and risk-taking.

Its share of the market fell from 7 per cent in 1960 to 3·7 per cent in 1965, and it seemed likely to be displaced from fourth place in the market, behind the three giants, by Volkswagen. It is not clear to what extent American Motors' position might have been eased if, as George Romney, former president of the company (later Governor of Michigan and a leading figure in the Republican Party), frequently urged, General Motors and Ford had been broken up by the Government into their constituent divisions. There is a strong feeling among dedicated trust-busters that the huge size of General Motors is somehow bad for the industry, and it will certainly be regretted by everyone (not least by General Motors itself) if American Motors is unable to survive. But it would be difficult to ascribe American Motors' difficulties to any specific monopolistic practice on the part of General Motors. The actual performance of G.M., and its record of service to the public, would hardly seem to justify an attempt to break it up. Some have suggested that G.M. should voluntarily spin off, say, the Chevrolet division as a separate company, but this suggestion is not likely to be acted upon. The vast size of the company may be objectionable on social or political grounds, but it has achieved its dominance by its own consistently good management, not by anti-competitive practices; the management of Ford and Chrysler, by contrast, has been erratic.

The significance of the antitrust laws has been to stimulate price competition and to act as a restraint on market power. They have not prevented some firms from growing to enormous size (principally through mergers), and from acquiring considerable power. Until the past decade, indeed, the anti-merger provisions were virtually ignored. Any attempt to dissolve these giant enterprises, to 'unscramble the corporate omelette', would almost certainly be resisted not only by the business community, but by the public as a whole. For this reason some Americans have lost faith in the antitrust laws and have proposed that firms of a certain size should be subjected to some form of public supervision; their prices might have to be justified before a public review board, or they might have to obtain Federal incorporation (instead of obtaining their charters from the states) which would involve certain rules and obligations. America's experience with the public regulation of private industry (described in the next chapter) is so unsatisfactory that these proposals have commanded little support. In a sense the periodic industrial investigations by Congressional Committees provide a way in which large firms are forced to answer for their actions. The House and Senate Small Business Committees frequently study merger trends and the difficulties of small businessmen, while the Senate Antitrust Subcommittee, particularly under the chairmanship of the late Senator Kefauver, has been a thorn in the side of firms like General Motors and U.S. Steel, forcing them to answer questions about pricing and investment policies and unearthing many hidden facts about their operations. The pressure of public opinion is a genuine restraint on big business, and the Congressional investigations help to keep the public better informed. In addition, there is always the possibility of extra-legal intervention by the Administration, which may take the form of public denunciation (as in the steel episode of April 1962) or, more commonly, of behind-the-scenes persuasion.

The result is a compromise between the traditional faith in the autonomous forces of the marketplace and the acceptance of an unavoidable degree of market power. Recent trends in antitrust law enforcement have involved a more vigorous attack on market power and a more hostile attitude towards 'bigness'. Some businessmen complain that the real purpose of the antitrust laws is being distorted by an excessive solicitude for small business. Even if their demands for a full-scale review of the laws are not satisfied, it is possible that changes in the composition of the Supreme Court will shift the emphasis in a different direction. But unless the American people are prepared to 'accept the direction of the few', strong antitrust weapons are necessary to keep the power of large firms within bounds.

4 · Government Regulation

The Regulators

THE enforcement of competition is one way in which the government can stimulate efficient performance in industry. The antitrust laws are an imperfect instrument, but an essential one. But there are important sectors of the economy where the antitrust laws are of limited relevance, and where other forms of government intervention have been devised. In every community there is only one telephone company, one gas company, one electric power company. These are the so-called natural monopolies where unrestricted competition between rival suppliers is impracticable. The companies fall into the category of public utilities to which the government, national or local, gives a franchise to perform a particular service to the public; in return for the absence of competition, the government regulates the company's performance so that its prices are reasonable and its service adequate.

The United States relies heavily on privately owned, publicly regulated companies to provide essential services in the fields of fuel and power, transport, and communications. Though there have sometimes been proposals to nationalize the railways and the electricity supply industry, government ownership is much less widespread than in other industrialized countries; public regulation is America's substitute for nationalization. Some fifteen per cent of the nation's power supply comes from Federally-owned bodies like the Tennessee Valley Authority, and, at the distribution end, about thirteen per cent of the nation's ultimate customers for electricity are served by local municipal systems. Many cities own and operate their own internal bus and rail services, but all inter-city transport services are provided by private companies. Although the postal system is the responsibility of the Federal Government, the nation's telephone system is privately owned.

Similarly, the exploitation of natural resources, including fuel, is left to private companies, but they, too, operate under some form of Government regulation. There is competition among oil companies and among coal producers, among railway companies and among airlines, among radio and television stations, but all these industries are, in one degree or another, 'affected with the public interest', and their activities are subjected to some form of public supervision. The national interest requires that the provision of transport, energy, and communications should be carried out as economically as possible. While the steel industry, for example, is supposed to regulate itself by competition (enforced by the antitrust laws), competition in these other industries has to be supplemented and in some cases replaced by public control.

In assuming partial responsibility for protecting the public interest in these industries, the Federal Government has adopted its usual pragmatic approach. By tradition the United States has avoided centralizing power, whether the power is privately or publicly held; the antitrust laws reflect the same attitude as the dislike of nationalization. Some degree of central planning, however, is essential in the fields of transport, energy, and communications. The problem has been to reconcile the need for planning with the belief in competition, private ownership and the decentralization of power.

Public regulation is carried out partly by state commissions, partly by Federal regulatory agencies – principally the Interstate Commerce Commission, for rail, road, and waterway transport, the Civil Aeronautics Board for airlines, the Federal Power Commission for gas pipelines and electricity supply, and the Federal Communications Commission for the telephone, telegraph, and broadcasting industries. Since most of the regulated companies operate across state boundaries, the Federal agencies have tended to assume greater importance, though the state commissions still play a major role in regulating local rates and conditions of service.

The performance of the Federal agencies has been unsatisfactory. Their difficulties stem from several factors. First, their status as 'independent' commissions between the executive branch of

Government (the Administration) and the legislative branch (the Congress) is ill-defined. While the members of the commissions are appointed by the President, their funds are provided by Congress, and their activities are continuously scrutinized by the relevant Congressional Committee; in some cases the chairman of the Congressional Committee seems to exert more power over the industry than the chairman of the commission itself. There is a tendency for Congress to pass unsolved questions to the commissions, but when the commission attempts to act independently, it may be instructed not to do so by the Congressional Committee. This happened, for example, when the Federal Communications Commission proposed to make compulsory on the broadcasting industry the limits on the number of commercials in each hour of broadcasting which had been recommended by the industry's own trade association.

Second, just as the Congressional Committee may be more concerned with the interests of the regulated industry than with the public interest, so the commissioners tend to acquire an industry orientation; the regulatees sometimes seem to become the regulators. In the early days of the Interstate Commerce Commission the railway owners found no difficulty in using it for their own ends, while the mere existence of the commission helped to satisfy the public clamour for Government supervision of the industry. Partly because sufficient expertise is not available elsewhere, members of the commissions have sometimes been drawn from the industry being regulated. There have even been suggestions that the industry should nominate its own list of candidates for the President to choose from. Similarly, the industry can exert great influence on Congress to reject a nominee who, in the industry's view, is hostile. While this industry orientation does not often lead to unethical conduct, it creates a climate of opinion in which it is hard for commissioners to take an independent and objective view of the public interest.

Third, the staff of the commissions is often inadequate in number and in quality, and the administrative procedures are so cumbersome that it may take several years before a case is disposed of. Some of the agencies have an ever-growing backlog of undecided cases. Mergers in a regulated industry may take two or three years to be approved by the agency, quite apart from possible objections on antitrust grounds from the Justice Department. The economics of an industry like natural gas may be distorted for years because of the Federal Power Commission's inability to decide on the right basis for fixing prices. The complexity of detailed price regulation, and the difficulty of establishing a 'fair' rate of return, have been the principal obstacles for both state and Federal regulatory commissions.

Fourth, and most important, the mandate under which the commissions operate is often unclear; major policy decisions which should have been taken by the Government are left in the air. As a result, the commissions tend to operate on a hand-to-mouth basis, dealing with problems as they arise and trying to find remedies for them, instead of looking to the future and forestalling problems before they arise. Major issues, such as the degree of competition that should prevail in the airline industry, are handled inconsistently, with the C.A.B. now favouring maximum competition and now favouring the consolidation of the industry into fewer systems. The effect on an industry of impending technical developments, like the introduction of large, high-speed jet airliners, rarely figures in the agency's forward planning. Forward planning, indeed, is conspicuous by its absence.

There is scope for improvement within the agencies. It may be desirable, for example, that each agency should make a periodic full-scale review of its work, as the Securities and Exchange Commission did in 1963 and 1964. But, in the absence of a clear and consistent national policy for the industry concerned, the commissions are obliged to pay more attention to individual cases than to the industry as a whole. The formulation of such a policy, moreover, often covers a much wider field than the single industry with which the agency is concerned. A policy for the railways depends on a national transport policy. A policy for the oil industry depends on a national energy policy. The costs of not having a policy for these crucial sectors of the economy may be heavy.

Problems in Transport

The responsibility for managing the nation's transport system is divided between private companies and Federal regulatory agencies. The Federal Government has relied partly on central planning, partly on competition, to provide the transport system which the national economy requires, but in doing so it seems to have got the worst of both worlds. Its central planning has not been detailed or comprehensive enough to ensure the development of each mode of transport in accordance with its economic capabilities. Competition has been inhibited by Government control of rates, which has often prevented an industry from competing for the sort of traffic that it could carry most economically. Regulatory policies were allowed to continue even after they had been made obsolete by technological or commercial changes. Until very recently the rate-making practices of the railways were controlled as if they still had the virtual monopoly of freight transport which they enjoyed in the early years of the century.

The investment of Government funds has played a crucial part in the development of the American transport system, but just as the regulatory system has tended to treat each industry separately, so large investments have been made in certain areas of transport without much consideration of their impact on other sectors. Public investment in transport, according to an official report,

has been guided by inadequate standards of analysis to assess cost in relation to benefit, has lacked any semblance of coordinated analysis among the several primary areas of investment, so that the relationships between them have been ignored, and has failed to take account of the adverse effect of new developments upon existing forms of transport, or in the alternative to consider whether like advantage could be secured at less cost through improvement of existing systems of transport.[1]

The report concluded that, 'were all traffic distributed in accordance with the true comparative advantage of the several forms of transport, the annual transport bill would be reduced by several billions of dollars on freight alone'.[2]

The early development of the railways was aided by Government grants of land to the railway promoters. In the 1920s the Government began to invest on a large scale in the construction of roads, waterways, and airway and airport facilities. At the present time the Government is engaged on a huge road-building programme, which is already having a profound effect on the railways. This is the 41,000-mile Interstate Highway System, due for completion in 1972 at a cost of some $50,000 million, which will blanket the country with high-speed motorways open to trucks as well as cars, linking every major city.

As in Britain and most other industrial countries, the development of these rival forms of transport has resulted in a contraction of the railway industry. As Table 1 shows, the railways' share of inter-city freight traffic fell sharply between 1940 and 1960. It was clear that the railway network was too large for the demands that were likely to be placed upon it. Although some companies went out of business and some lines were shut down, there was still a considerable duplication of facilities, so that railway companies were cutting each other's throats at a time when the cream of their business was being taken away by rival forms of transport. The need for consolidation was in fact recognized as an object of public policy as early as 1920. During the next forty years a host of proposals were put forward for creating a small number of large regional railway companies or even for merging the whole system into a single corporation which could either be privately owned and publicly regulated (like the American Telephone and Telegraph Company in the telephone industry) or publicly owned by the Government. (The railways had been run by the Government as an emergency measure during the First World War.) But the old fear of the railways as ruthless monopolists has persisted; there has always been strenuous opposition, on antitrust grounds, to any proposal that would create fewer and larger companies in the industry.

The deteriorating finances of the railways, and the danger of the wholesale abandonment of service in some areas, have gradually brought about a change in public policy. In the last few years an attempt has been made to bring the regulatory system up to date and to evolve a new set of policies for transport as a whole, which would stimulate rather than hamper the development of the industry. Although there has been strong resistance from the motor and water carriers, some steps have been taken to free the

TABLE 1
Volume of inter-city freight traffic (millions of ton-miles)

	Railways	Motor vehicles	Inland waterways	Oil pipelines
1940	379,000 (61·3%)	62,000 (10%)	118,000 (19·1%)	59,000 (9·6%)
1950	597,000 (56·2%)	173,000 (16·3%)	163,000 (15·4%)	129,000 (12·1%)
1960	579,000 (44·1%)	285,000 (21·7%)	220,000 (16·8%)	229,000 (17·4%)
1964	666,000 (43·5%)	347,000 (22·7%)	250,000 (16·3%)	266,000 (17·5%)

Volume of inter-city passenger traffic (millions of passenger-miles)

	Railways	Buses	Inland waterways	Airlines
1940	25,000 (67·1%)	9,800 (26·5%)	1,317 (3·6%)	1,052 (2·8%)
1950	33,000 (46·3%)	26,000 (37·7%)	1,190 (1·7%)	10,100 (14·3%)
1960	22,000 (27·8%)	20,000 (25·7%)	2,068 (2·7%)	34,000 (43·8%)

railways from minimum-rate regulation on at least part of their tonnage. The objective, not yet achieved, is a neutral regulatory system which would encourage competition between the modes and not impose special handicaps on any one industry.

In addition there has been a much more liberal policy on the part of the Government towards railway mergers. Several important mergers have been approved by the Interstate Commerce Commission. The most important consolidation move, involving the two great Eastern companies, the New York Central and the Pennsylvania, is on the way towards completion; this will be the biggest merger in the history of American business. The objections of the trust-busters to the creation of such a colossus will be overruled on the ground that competition from other forms of transport (reinforced, of course, by Government supervision) will provide a sufficient constraint.

As Government policy towards the railways has become more liberal, a new competitive spirit has emerged in the industry itself. A host of managerial, technical and marketing innovations has been introduced, which, while they will not re-establish the industry's former dominance, are already recovering a significant proportion of the traffic lost to the waterways and the road-haulage industry. High-speed 'piggyback' services, in which trailers are carried on flat wagons, have won back long-haul traffic. The development of three-level carriers has recaptured the business of carrying cars from Detroit to the major markets. Permanently coupled unit trains for bulk cargoes such as coal, operating on almost a shuttle basis, have made dramatic savings in costs. The use of electronic systems for centralized traffic control has improved the utilization of the industry's equipment. The old rate-making principle, whereby charges were based on the supposed value of the service to the customer rather than on the costs of supplying the service, is gradually being abandoned. Like many of the industries described in Chapter 2, the railways have begun to lose their preoccupation with 'production' and to concentrate on marketing.

The road hauliers and the water carriers, of course, have not been idle. Bigger barges and longer trailers have been developed; their costs, too, are coming down. The rapid development of pipelines for bulk commodities, even for such an apparently solid commodity as coal, has been another important competitive factor. But for high-value manufactured products the inherent advantages of the railways in long-distance, line-haul operations are becoming more widely recognized. With the development of containers that can be freely interchanged from one mode of transport to another, it seems likely that the railways' prime role will be to act as wholesalers, specializing in long-distance journeys, while the road hauliers will play more of a retailing function, specializing in terminal operations and in the delivery of goods to the final customer.

The gradual modernization of the railway industry has involved serious conflicts between management and labour. (Britain's problems over the introduction of liner trains have been very similar.) During the long years of decline inefficient manning practices were allowed to become established by complacent or incompetent managers. As the number of jobs in the industry steadily fell, the railwaymen who remained were even more adamant in their opposition to any changes in work rules which would result in smaller train crews. Until recently the employers made little attempt to change the situation; the industry became a byword for 'featherbedding'. But in the last few years considerable progress has been made, with the Federal Government acting as mediator between the two sides. The cost to the companies of buying out restrictive practices has been very heavy, but they are now in a much better position to increase productivity.

The Government has contributed to the industry's revival by relaxing regulatory restrictions and by assisting in the settlement of its labour problems. In the future the Government may try to play a more active role in stimulating technical change in the industry, by using its purchasing power, for example, to insist on the most modern transportation techniques. Early in 1966 President Johnson proposed the creation of a new Department of Transportation to coordinate the work of the various transport agencies.

There are some important regulatory problems left unsolved. The extent to which the road hauliers should contribute to the cost of the Government's road-building programme is one major bone of contention. There is still too little coordination between the various regulatory agencies; there have been cases where the Interstate Commerce Commission has permitted a railway company to abandon passenger service between two cities, while the Civil Aeronautics Board has agreed to subsidize an airline service on the same route. Although the 'trunk' airlines, operating on the densely travelled routes between the big cities, are able to operate without a subsidy, the local and regional airlines (together with a small number of helicopter operators) are still partly dependent on Government funds. Strenuous efforts are being made to reduce the subsidy; the Government, for example, has tried to foster the development of a more economical small airliner.

In other sectors of transport, too, there are signs of a greater determination on the Government's part to ensure that it gets an adequate return on its investment. There has been, for example, a reappraisal of the subsidy programme for the American shipping industry. The promotion of an American merchant marine, large enough to handle the nation's foreign trade and to serve as a naval or military auxiliary in time of war, began with the Shipping Act of 1916, but it soon became clear that, because of their high construction and operating costs, American ships could not compete on equal terms with foreign vessels. Hence in 1936 a new programme of Federal aid was started, providing for the payment of a construction-differential subsidy and an operating-differential subsidy to enable American shipowners to match the costs of their foreign competitors. These subsidies are granted to the common carrier or liner operators which sail between fixed ports or ranges of ports on regular schedules; in 1964 this fleet consisted of about four hundred cargo liners and thirty passenger and combination vessels. Direct subsidies are not paid to the tramp ships or bulk carriers that operate on a contract basis, but they share in an indirect subsidy provided by the cargo preference laws, which require that at least 50 per cent of all Government-financed cargoes (chiefly foreign aid and military shipments) must be carried in U.S.-flag ships. The tramp fleet has been declining steadily since the war, and now comprises about a hundred and ten vessels. Even more drastic has been the decline of the U.S.-flag tanker fleet, which now comprises about thirty-five vessels; the international oil companies place most of their orders with foreign shipyards, and the domestic fleet is likely to disappear unless the Government decides to preserve it for reasons of national security.

The cost to the taxpayer of maintaining a large subsidized fleet has been rising steadily; the operating subsidy now runs at about $200 million a year and the construction subsidy at about $100 million a year. At the same time, the share of the subsidized fleet in the carriage of America's imports and exports has been declining. Since the war the percentage of America's exports carried in U.S.-flag ships has dropped from 65 per cent to 10 per cent. Their dependence on Federally-financed cargoes has also grown; 45 per cent of the liner ships' cargo in 1962 was Government financed, and the dependence of tramp ships and tankers on the Government was even greater. It has been argued that, apart from considerations of prestige and possible security requirements, the existence of a subsidized merchant fleet makes little net contribution to the national economy. Moreover, the operation of the subsidy does not help the American shipowner to make the kind of investment in machinery and equipment that might eventually close the gap between U.S. and foreign costs. Under the subsidy programme, it is to the American's advantage to economize on those factors of production which are most expensive in the countries of his competitors, principally capital, and not to economize on those factors which are most expensive in the United States, particularly labour.[3]

Widespread dissatisfaction with the mounting costs of the programme, coupled with the realization that national security requirements in the nuclear age might be very different from the past, has led to a reappraisal of the programme. In 1965 there were suggestions that the Government might eliminate the ship construction subsidies, call a halt to future passenger liner construction, and replace the cargo preference law (which involves an indirect subsidy of about $80 million a year) with an incentive subsidy designed to encourage automation of subsidized ships. There has been some progress in the mechanization of American ships; most of the leading companies have automation programmes in hand. On the horizon, too, is the possibility of an automated, nuclear-powered fleet which might enable the American shipowner to match foreign costs. The shipping unions are beginning to realize that their own survival depends on an accelerated modernization programme, despite the reduction in manning which it will entail. The Federal Government has made it clear that subsidies will only continue if management and labour press ahead with automation, so that the costs of the programme can be controlled and eventually reduced.

Whatever the response, it is clear that some form of Government subsidy is essential to the survival of the American shipping industry. The same may apply to the railways' passenger services. For although the railways' freight prospects are improving, most of them are still making heavy losses on passenger traffic; it is not at all clear what combination of public and private policies will solve the problem. In inter-city passenger traffic the railways have been hard hit by the airlines and, of course, by the private car. As the Government's highway programme continues, pressure for abandonment of railway passenger services will be intensified. Lower prices and improved service may be able to attract sufficient traffic on routes that are not long enough to give an obvious edge to the airlines, but there is a growing belief that, if the public interest requires the continued existence of long-distance rail passenger services, they will have to be underwritten or subsidized by the Government. In the densely populated North East, the Government has already provided funds for research into the possible development of high-speed rail services between Boston, New York and Washington.

Within the cities the problems are even more severe, and the need for Government assistance more obvious. Although there are a few examples of successful commuter railway operations, notably in Chicago, most of them are unprofitable, chiefly because their heavy investment in plant and personnel is utilized only for two brief periods at the beginning and end of the day. Many urban motorways have been built, and it may be possible to develop bus commutation as a partial substitute both for railway services and for private cars; more use may be made of discriminatory charges on road users so as to discourage single-passenger car travel, especially during the rush-hour periods.

In the metropolitan regions of the country there is gradual progress towards the coordination of transport policy. The Federal Government has provided funds to aid local communities work out their public transport problems, and they are being encouraged to formulate integrated plans for their regions. In most of the largest cities, the railways will probably remain the most economical form of commuter transport; cities which lack such facilities, such as Los Angeles and Washington, are taking steps to develop them. But many of the commuter railway companies, though privately owned, are heavily subsidized by local taxpayers; in New York there is a possibility that one of the most important companies, the Long Island Rail Road, will be taken over and operated by the state government. Regional transport planning is complicated, too, by the lack of adequate planning machinery. In the New York City area, for example, the commuters come from three states – New York, New Jersey, and Connecticut – and cooperation between the state governments is often difficult to achieve.

Thus there are many transport problems still to be overcome in the United States. Just as nationalization in Britain has failed to correct the structural defects in the transport industry, so America's system of public regulation has created rigidities which have impeded the efficient development of the various sectors of the industry. In both countries progress towards a more rational arrangement has involved conflicts with vested interests in management, in the unions, and in government itself. In the future it seems likely that the American Government will switch its efforts away from detailed rate regulation towards more positive measures for stimulating efficiency, partly by encouraging competition between the modes, partly by ensuring that its own expenditures are directed towards the health of the transport industry as a whole.

The High Cost of Energy

Just as Americans are paying a higher price for transport than they need, so the price of fuel and power could be reduced if the supply arrangements were organized more rationally. In the oil industry, in particular, prices are kept artificially high, partly by the conservation programmes adopted by most producing states, partly by restrictions on imports.

The production of oil, an exhaustible natural resource that is clearly 'affected with the public interest', is in the hands of private companies, but the Federal Government and the state governments intervene in the industry to prevent unnecessary waste. It was unfortunate that, at the start, the 'law of capture' was applied to oil so that the owner of a tract of land acquired the title to all the oil that could be obtained from wells on his tract, even though part or all of the oil might flow from a reservoir under an adjoining tract. To be efficiently exploited, the reservoir or 'pool' should have been treated as a whole, but proposals for the compulsory unitization of pools have generally been resisted.

Recognizing the need for some production controls, most state governments have adopted various forms of 'pro-rationing', whereby each well is allotted a certain daily production on the basis of the estimated national demand for oil; the estimate of national demand is made by the Bureau of Mines, part of the Department of the Interior, and shared out among the producing states. This has encouraged companies to drill wells in areas where the existence of an oil pool is already established, so that they can obtain more 'allowables' from the state authorities. There is an unnecessary amount of development drilling in proven areas, and there has been a steady decline in exploratory drilling in unproven areas; for if a new well is found in virgin territory, it can only be produced at a fraction of its capacity, and the risk and cost of finding it may be wasted.

The pro-rationing system keeps prices up and high-cost wells in production, while the prolific, low-cost wells have to operate far below capacity. The system is reinforced by restrictions on oil imports from Venezuela, the Middle East, and other countries where production costs are much lower; imported oil, costing at least $1 a barrel less than domestic supplies, is restricted to 20 per cent of the market. On conservation grounds, it would be logical to permit the free importation of oil, so that domestic oil resources could be made to last longer. But it has been argued that an active oil-producing industry is essential to national security, and that free imports would destroy the industry. It is obviously important to know how much of the industry could survive in the face of unrestricted imports, so that the restrictions are no greater than they need be. But this calculation has been neglected. The industry is protected against imports ostensibly on national security grounds, but in practice the import quota system is not much different from any other protectionist device used to shield an inefficient domestic industry from the rigours of competition.

The cost of the pro-rationing system and the import controls has been estimated at about $4,000 million a year. Fortunately, oil is not the country's only indigenous fuel. Although the Government has sometimes intervened to support coal prices and to protect the industry against competition from cheap fuel oil, the production and sale of coal has, for the most part, been left to private companies. America's coal seams are rich and easily mined, but the industry is also highly efficient; this is one of the principal reasons why, despite her oil policies, the United States has enjoyed lower energy costs than most other industrial nations.

The coal industry is mostly in the hands of large companies, which, encouraged by the United Mine Workers' Union, have invested heavily in mechanization and continuous mining equipment. Between 1952 and 1962 productivity increased from 7·47 to 14·72 tons per man-day; the pit-head price of coal is less than

TABLE 2

Energy production 1940–60 (millions of tons, coal equivalent)

	Coal	Oil	Natural gas	Water power
1940	511 (53%)	300 (31%)	115 (12%)	34 (4%)
1950	559 (42%)	437 (33%)	261 (20%)	60 (5%)
1960	416 (27%)	570 (36%)	528 (33%)	66 (4%)

half what it is in Britain. As Table 2 shows, coal's share of the energy market has been declining, largely because of the advance of natural gas, but it has remained the dominant fuel for electricity generation and by 1980 its share of this market is expected to be even larger. Coal's future depends partly on continued mechanization of the mines, partly on further economies in the transportation of coal from mine to consumer. The threat of nuclear energy, coal pipelines, and extra high-voltage transmission has spurred the railways to look for new techniques, such as the 'unit train' in which trainload lots of coal are shipped from one mine or group of mines to one power station. The possibility of high-speed automated trains, operating a shuttle service between mine and power station, is also being considered. This is a subject to which the new generation of railway managers is devoting considerable attention.

One of coal's main rivals, the nuclear power industry, has depended heavily on the Federal Government. Public money was needed, as it was in the early days of the railways and the airlines, to guide a new technology into commercial application. 'The proper role of the Government', according to the Atomic Energy Commission, 'is to take the lead in developing and demonstrating the technology in such ways that economic factors will promote industrial applications in the public interest and lead to a self-sustaining and growing nuclear power industry'.[4]

By 1965 both the utilities which produce electric power and the manufacturers of generating equipment, notably General Electric and Westinghouse, had accumulated considerable experience in the construction and operation of nuclear power stations. The prices quoted by General Electric in its successful bid for the Oyster Creek plant in New Jersey suggest that within a few years nuclear power stations will be competitive with conventional stations in most parts of the country. But the Oyster Creek contract has spurred the coal producers, backed by the railway companies, to find ways of cutting their own costs even further. Competition between the different fuels has played a significant part in bringing power costs down. This, of course, has also happened in the U.K., but the Americans may have benefited from another competitive element which has not been present in the U.K. In the United States the decisions on fuels to be used for electricity generation have not been taken by a single organization like the Central Electricity Generating Board, but by a large number of individual utilities. The existence of these independent centres of initiative has, for example, encouraged several different approaches to the problem of producing nuclear power economically.

It has been estimated that nuclear power will account for about thirteen per cent of the nation's generating capacity by 1980. It is not clear how fast the high capital costs of nuclear power stations will be reduced, or how serious the problems of safety and waste disposal will turn out to be. Competitors have argued that the subsidies which the nuclear power industry has received and is still receiving from the Federal Government, especially in the field of research and development, are placing them at an unfair disadvantage. There have been allegations, too, that the equipment suppliers are 'buying' their way into the business by quoting unrealistically low prices for atomic power stations, and that true economic factors are being distorted.

Another complicating factor was the eagerness, on the part of the privately-owned utilities and the equipment suppliers, to avoid any Government involvement in the generation of commercial nuclear power. The spectre of another Tennessee Valley Authority for nuclear power haunted them. (It was perhaps surprising that the existing T.V.A., and the other publicly-owned utilities, played so passive a role in the development of nuclear power.) These additional factors made it difficult for the nation's future energy requirements to be accurately assessed.

The unending feud between the 'private' and 'public' sectors of the electricity supply industry has had harmful consequences. There are about 400 investor-owned utility systems (serving 79 per cent of the nation's total ultimate consumers), about 2,200 local public agency systems, about 1,000 cooperative systems, and several large Federal systems including the Tennessee Valley Authority in the south east and the Bonneville Power Administration in the north west. The development of public power during the New Deal was viewed by its promoters, not as the precursor to nationalization, but as a device for regulating private utilities, competing against them and bringing their rates down. The T.V.A. was especially successful in this respect; it was used as a 'yardstick', by which the adequacy of private suppliers' rates and service could be judged. But the development of public power was bitterly resisted by the private utilities and cooperation between the two sectors of the industry has consequently been difficult.

The need for such cooperation has become increasingly apparent as the economies to be derived from pooling and interconnexions, leading to an eventual 'national grid', were realized. A substantial amount of voluntary pooling took place, but neither the state utility commissions nor the Federal Power Commission could compel it. In its National Power Survey completed in 1964 the F.P.C. estimated that consumer electricity prices could be reduced by an average of 27 per cent by 1980 if all sections of the industry agreed to undertake a massive coordination programme. The serious power failure which occurred in New York and other parts of the north east in November 1965 seemed likely to support the F.P.C.'s requests for more authority to bring about interconnexions between neighbouring electric power systems.

The problem is how to reconcile the advantages of having independent centres of initiative in the electricity supply industry with the advantages of coordination. Conceivably the nation's electricity prices would have been lower if the supply industry had been in the hands of a single nation-wide organization along the lines of the American Telephone and Telegraph Company in the telephone industry. But the telephone company is an exception which runs counter to the general American distaste for the centralization of power. Given a more rational and less dogmatic attitude on the part of the two sides in the public–private power controversy, it should be possible to achieve the degree of coordination that is desirable. Whether the Federal Power Commission will need more effective controls over the industry to achieve this result remains to be seen.

Communications

The outstanding example of successful planning and coordination from the centre is the nation's telephone system, where the service to the public has probably been reduced in cost and improved in quality more continuously and effectively than in any other industry. The task of regulating the telephone industry is shared between the Federal Communications Commission, which supervises long-distance, interstate telephone rates, and the state public utilities commissions, which are responsible for intrastate rates. But the most important fact about this industry, and probably the principal reason for its outstanding performance, is that it is dominated by a single, highly efficient enterprise. The American Telephone and Telegraph Company, which with its affiliated companies operates the Bell System, is responsible for over 80 per cent of local telephone service and an even larger proportion of long-distance service. It has been described as 'the largest aggregation of capital and resources that has ever been controlled by a single private company at any time in the history of business'. Not only is it a public utility providing telephone service to the public, but it has a powerful manufacturing arm, Western Electric, which ranks among the top ten industrial corporations in the country, and a research arm, Bell Laboratories, which is widely regarded as the most productive private research organization in the world; the invention of the transistor is its best-known accomplishment.

The efficiency of the American telephone system, which is the envy of the world, is due not so much to the effectiveness of public regulation as to the skill of the men who manage the Bell System. The achievement would not have been possible without the acceptance by Congress of the principle of a privately-owned, publicly-regulated telephone monopoly, but it cannot be said that the actual practice of regulation has contributed significantly to the industry's progress. Like other utilities, the Bell System and its subsidiary companies frequently disagree with the F.C.C. and the state commissions over the level of telephone rates, but it has been able, through its own profits and by raising capital from the public, to finance massive investments in equipment and research. There have been doubts about the size of the enterprise – whether it is right for the United States to permit the existence of so powerful a private organization. To counter these fears the Bell System has endeavoured to demonstrate, partly by its public relations activities but mostly by its performance, that monopoly in this industry is good. 'Our goal', says Frederick Kappel, president of the company, 'is to conduct our business in such a manner that our customers will see in the result, in our line of goods and services, all the virtues of competition, in addition to all the values of a single, interconnected service.'[5] There have been attempts to force the Bell System to divorce itself from Western Electric, but the only major concession to the antitrust laws was the company's agreement, in 1913, to relinquish control of Western Union; the company had previously argued that its business should logically include telegraph as well as telephone communications.

Despite this gap, which, in view of Western Union's subsequent difficulties, may have been a blessing in disguise, the managers of the Bell System have been able to view the field of communications as a whole, and to define their own goals in simple terms – to provide the best possible communications service at the lowest cost, consistent with the health of the enterprise. 'In the Bell System,' Kappel has said, 'our continuous purpose has been to find and use every resource that will contribute to the advancement of communications.' Scientists, engineers and salesmen – all members of the organization are devoted to this single task. The company is able to apply the 'systems concept' to the communications industry largely because its own business is so obviously a system and has to be viewed as a whole. The combination in a single organization of research, production and sales, coupled with a rigorous attention to standards of performance in all parts of the enterprise, has been remarkably successful. Internal discipline appears to be an effective substitute for external competitive pressures.

In another aspect of communications, Government regulation has been less successful. This is the field of radio and television. Here the Federal Communications Commission is not concerned with rates but it controls the issuance and renewal of licences to operate radio and television broadcasting stations. This is based on the principle that the airwaves are public property and that operators of radio stations are 'affected with the public interest'. As Mr Herbert Hoover, then Secretary of Commerce, said in 1920:

Radio is not to be considered merely as a business carried on for private gain, for private advertisement, or for the entertainment of the curious. It is to be considered as a public concern, impressed with a public trust, and to be considered primarily from the standpoint of public interest.

The difficulty has been that the 'public interest' in broadcasting has never been clearly defined, and broadcasting stations are operated for private profit, financed out of advertising revenue, and not, as in the case of the British Broadcasting Corporation, out of fees paid by the listeners. Very few stations have had their licences revoked, and then usually for fraud rather than for neglecting the public interest in broadcasting.

As the industry developed, the three 'networks' – Columbia Broadcasting System, National Broadcasting Company, and American Broadcasting Company – which own a few stations of their own, but principally supply programmes to affiliated stations throughout the country, began to assume much greater importance than the individual stations, but they were not subject to the F.C.C.'s authority.

The familiar criticism of the industry is that programme content is dictated by the advertiser, and that the objective is mass entertainment at the expense of 'public service' broadcasting, which would include documentary films and 'cultural' programmes. While the broadcasters argue that their responsibility to the public is synonymous with their responsibility to the advertiser, critics complain that 'the tail of merchandising wags the dog of broadcasting in the public interest', and that the interests of the seller, the advertiser, inevitably take precedence over those of the buyer, the public. It has sometimes been suggested that the Government should establish a Tennessee Valley Authority in broadcasting, a publicly-financed network which would set standards and provide competition for the commercial carriers. To some extent the Government has supported the growth of educational TV stations, which may eventually develop into a fourth network, but so far only a few stations exist and their finances are generally precarious. There have been hopes that Pay-TV, where the subscriber pays for the programmes he watches, might prove an effective rival to advertiser-sponsored television, but a recent Pay-TV operation in California ran into difficulties, partly because of organized opposition from cinema owners, partly because of a disappointing public response.

The only major attempt by the Government to alter the economics of the industry was to compel the TV set manufacturers (in 1962) to make all new sets capable of receiving not only Very High Frequency broadcasts but also Ultra High Frequency broadcasts. Most existing sets were capable of receiving only the twelve V.H.F. channels; because these channels were already very crowded, an extension of U.H.F. broadcasting was the only possible way of providing new competition for the existing networks. It is not yet clear to what extent U.H.F. channels will be used by newcomers to the broadcasting industry, or whether the three existing networks will also dominate the U.H.F. field. The Government presumably hopes that an increase in competition, rather than an increase in public control, will help to turn the industry from the 'vast wasteland' which one chairman of the F.C.C. considered it to be into a medium which effectively serves the public interest.

The inability of the Federal Communications Commission to impose its will on the broadcasting industry reflects two basic problems from which several of the regulatory agencies suffer – the failure to adjust the regulatory system to take account of new commercial developments (in this case, the emergence of the networks as the dominant forces in the industry), and the uneasy relationship between the regulators and Congress. The broadcasters have always wielded great influence in Congress, partly because politicians depend on them for free 'exposure' to the public during election campaigns. Whenever the F.C.C. proposes new rules which would limit the broadcaster's freedom of action, there is a tendency for members of Congress to bring pressure on the Commission to abandon or modify their proposal. The influence of the Commission on the performance of the broadcasting industry has been, in consequence, very small.

5 · Is Wall Street Irrelevant?

Decline of the Owner-Manager

MOST large American companies are publicly owned, in the sense that any member of the public may purchase a share in them. Their shares are traded on one of the nation's stock exchanges, of which the New York Stock Exchange is the most important, or on the less formal and less closely regulated 'over-the-counter' market. Their shareholders are usually numerous and widely dispersed. American Telephone and Telegraph, the most popular stock with 'small investors', has over two million shareholders, and a figure of several hundred thousand for large companies is not uncommon. The men who manage the firm may also be shareholders, but it is becoming rare for them to hold more than a small proportion of the total stock outstanding. The nineteenth-century practice, where the owner either managed the firm himself or wielded a decisive influence in selecting and guiding the managers, has not disappeared, but is waning. Most large companies are run by professional managers, not by owner-managers.

What this means in practice is that the shareholders come to be regarded as one of several groups which have certain claims on the company and whose claims must be adequately satisfied. In theory, the authority of the shareholders is supreme, and 'making money for the shareholders' is the objective to which managers frequently pledge their loyalty. But because of their diffusion it is difficult for the shareholders to assert their authority, except in rare cases. When an outside group attempts to wrest control of the company from the existing management, the shareholders' votes are decisive. but these take-over battles are infrequent. A stockholder can sue the managers if he feels they are not fulfilling their responsibilities, but this is a costly process which often fails. He is more likely to express his displeasure by selling his shares, and investing in another company.

To keep the shareholders happy, the managers must normally

77

pay dividends that are regarded as reasonable in relation to the company's past performance and the performance of other companies, and the market price of its shares must rise at least in line with the market as a whole. (Some fast-growing firms, which need to plough back all their profits into the business, pay no dividends; but this is offset, for the shareholders, by a faster than average rise in the price of the shares.) If the dividend is cut and the market price falls, not only is the prestige of the company damaged, but it will be difficult for the managers to raise money from the public if the company's internal resources are insufficient to finance necessary or desirable capital investments. Most successful firms depend on internally generated funds (retained profits and depreciation) to finance the bulk of their expansion, but the future is unpredictable and recourse to the stock market may eventually be necessary. Hence a rising market price and a contented army of shareholders are always important.

Once the shareholders' claims are met, the managers have a considerable degree of discretion in deploying the company's resources. Most firms pay out some 50–60 per cent of their net profits in dividends. What is left is used in a way which, in the manager's view, will be of most value in furthering the company's long-term interests. To the extent that the retained earnings serve to enhance the company's worth, this will be reflected in the market price of its shares, and the shareholder will be happy.

But the interests of manager and stockholder do not necessarily always coincide. In seeking outlets for the profits that are retained in the business, the manager may be inclined to seek a rate of return which seems to be adequate and feasible in the light of the company's past performance. But the shareholder, if the money was his to dispose of, might find better investment opportunities, in other companies or in other industries, where the rate of return might be higher. At the same time managers are reluctant to pay out a larger proportion of the profits in dividends. For the wealthier investor the tax structure bears more heavily on dividend income than on the capital gains that are realized when he buys stock at one price and sells it at a higher price. The investor benefits from a high rate of retained earnings – some have even urged the abolition of dividends, so that the shareholders could take all their income in the form of capital gains – but at the expense of abdicating control over the deployment of the company's resources. Not only does the existing distribution of capital among corporations tend to be perpetuated, but the freedom of the managers from stockholders' supervision is increased. Some firms deliberately restrict their investments to what can be financed from internal sources. The recent introduction of the Corporation Tax in Britain, separating the taxation of companies from that of individuals, seems likely to have similar effects; by encouraging firms to retain and reinvest their earnings instead of distributing them in higher dividends, the tax may make their managers more independent of the shareholders.

The chief officers of the company can, in theory, be removed by the shareholders if their performance is unsatisfactory. 'Through the instrumentality of the ballot,' according to the official version, 'stockholders have effective control over management. They use this power in the election of directors and voting upon other important issues which are placed before them.' In practice, the management nominates a list of directors, and the election or re-election is usually a mere formality; this process has been compared to the elections that take place in totalitarian countries. Hence the directors of most large corporations come to resemble what has been called 'an automatic self-perpetuating oligarchy'.[1]

The apparent freedom of management from stockholder control has disturbing implications, and attempts have been made to resuscitate the owner-manager. There are, of course, a number of American corporations in which ownership interests play an important part. It is estimated that in 20 per cent of the 500 largest manufacturing companies there is a significant degree of family management or control.[2] They include such well-known and successful firms as Du Pont, Corning Glass, Firestone, Inland Steel, Gulf Oil and Ford. There are those who argue that firms in which 'partial proprietors' play an active managerial role tend to show a better performance than those in which professional managers have complete control.[3]

The consistently outstanding performance of Du Pont is a tribute to the effectiveness of family management (or at least to the effectiveness of this particular family), and its officers have always been champions of the view that 'interested owners' are essential for a firm's success. 'The professional manager', according to its president, 'will not have the same outlook as the owner-manager traditionally had. As steward of someone else's money, he will tend to be cautious, far more cautious, probably, than he should be. It will be hard for him to think beyond his own tenure. He will be interested in a safe performance over a decade or so; an owner-manager would look half a century ahead.' It is sometimes argued that if there is a powerful stockholder looking over the manager's shoulder, such as the Hanna interests in the case of Consolidation Coal and National Steel, or (until the recent Supreme Court ruling*) the Du Pont interests in the case of General Motors, the manager is likely to work 'extra hard'.

Similar arguments have been used to defend the sale of stock, sometimes at preferential prices, to the company's executives. It is thought that when the executive stands to benefit personally from higher profits, in the form of larger dividends and a rising share price, he, too, will work 'extra hard'. This argument is somewhat weakened by the use of stock-option schemes to reward an executive in a way which would minimize his tax liabilities. He is given the right to buy stock at a fixed price, and, if the price rises, he may realize a capital gain by selling it. Since the connexion between a rise in the market price of the stock and the performance of an individual executive is, at least in the short term, distant, these stock-option schemes have been much criticized; for although in the long run the price is likely to reflect the profit record and prospects of the company, there may be wide short-term fluctuations which stem from changes in the market as a whole and which provide opportunities for unmerited capital gains. Recent changes in taxation, by cutting ordinary income taxes and extending the minimum holding period for buyers of stock under stock-option schemes,

*See page 44.

have tended to switch the emphasis towards cash compensation as an incentive for management.[4]

In any case, the sale of stock to company executives does nothing to halt the diffusion of stock ownership. The fact that an executive holds stock in the company does not make him any more subject to the supervision and control of the mass of stockholders scattered throughout the country. Only if there is a dominant stockholder, whether it is a family or an individual, will the manager's freedom of action be significantly limited.

There are wealthy individuals who use their fortune to acquire control of a company, or a number of companies, and who take an active part in management. Such a man is Norton Simon, a Los Angeles businessman who in recent years has bought interests in several companies where management was laggard and opportunities for growth were being neglected. These 'corporate raiders' are sometimes motivated simply by personal greed or ambition, but men like Simon (who has been described as a builder and reformer rather than a raider) can play a useful role in breathing new life into badly managed companies and improving the efficiency of industry. It is interesting to note that, in choosing his targets, Simon generally selects companies in which share ownership is widely diffused; large shareholders, he thinks, are more likely to be committed to the existing managers of the firm and to resist attempts by an outsider to acquire a controlling interest.

But private fortunes, especially inherited ones, are diminishing in importance, and as companies grow in size the power of an individual stockholder tends to decline. The American economy might be more 'capitalistic' if there were more Norton Simons roaming the country; the threat of an attack from Simon will certainly make managers work 'extra hard' to satisfy their shareholders. But in practice such men are rare. The owner-manager is on the wane.

The Influence of Shareholders

The growing distance that separates manager from shareholder does not mean that the shareholder's interests can be ignored in the formulation of corporate policies. For one thing, the manager's obligations to the shareholder are laid down by law. The Securities and Exchange Commission, a government agency created in 1934, is responsible for protecting investors against misrepresentation and fraud and for ensuring that the necessary information is available to enable investors to make an informed judgement of the value of securities that they may purchase or hold. The S.E.C., for which there is as yet no counterpart in Britain, has authority both over shares that are listed on the stock exchanges and over the much larger number of shares traded in the 'over-the-counter' markets. In addition, the exchanges themselves, notably the New York Stock Exchange and the American Stock Exchange, have, under prodding from the S.E.C., taken further steps to ensure that their members – the broker-dealers who buy and sell shares for the public – pay more regard to the interests and frailties of investors. These exchanges are privately owned and managed, but the S.E.C. has succeeded in transforming them from 'private clubs' into responsible public institutions. 'Self-regulation' of the securities industry is still the preferred way, but the power of the S.E.C. ensures that the public interest in efficient and honest trading is maintained.

Because of this protection more information about publicly held corporations is available in the U.S. than in foreign countries, where sales figures, investments in other companies, and many essential facts are usually kept secret. Insistence on 'full disclosure' has effects that go beyond the securities industry itself. It enables the Press, for example, to comment more intelligently about the activities of large corporations. Most companies, having been compelled by law to disclose their activities to shareholders, have voluntarily adopted a policy of frankness towards other interested parties, including the newspapers. This may help to create a favourable 'image' of themselves in the eyes of the public, but it also enables the public to obtain a clearer understanding of companies whose activities have a considerable impact on the welfare of the nation as a whole.

In British industry, by contrast, there is a marked lack of

information on which the prospects of a company or an industry can be accurately assessed, though even Britain is a long way ahead of the Continent in this respect. In the British motor industry, for example, statistics about a manufacturer's sales and production schedules are often unobtainable; in the United States all the manufacturers publish such information on a monthly basis as a matter of course. This is one reason why the American business Press is so much better informed about industry than is the case in the United Kingdom. Journals like *Fortune, Business Week, Forbes Magazine*, and the *Wall Street Journal* provide an invaluable commentary on the inner workings of industry. It is perhaps significant that the British financial Press is generally superior to its American counterpart in the coverage of government economic policies; the activities of businessmen seem to count for less in Britain than the activities of government.

Contributing towards the fuller disclosure of company affairs in the United States has been the recent change in the composition of the share-owning population. While the number of individual shareholders has risen rapidly from 6·5 million in 1952 to an estimated 20 million in 1965, there has also been a remarkable growth in stock ownership by institutions, chiefly the insurance companies, the pension funds, and the mutual funds, which correspond to unit trusts in Britain. The growing desire for financial security has caused the assets of these institu-

TABLE 3
How savings institutions have grown
(total assets in millions of dollars)

	1929	1945	1962	Per cent increase 1945–62
Life Insurance Companies	17,482	44,797	133,291	198
Mutual Savings Banks	9,873	16,962	46,121	172
Savings and Loan Associations	8,695	8,747	93,816	973
Company Pension Funds	500	2,700	35,999	1,233
State and Local Govt Pensions Funds	424	2,615	24,300	829
Mutual Funds	134	1,284	22,950	1,687

tions to rise more rapidly than the economy as a whole during the past few decades. These institutions collect and allocate a substantial part of all savings by individuals. Most of the savings were until recently invested in fixed-interest securities, such as government bonds, but the inflationary climate that followed the end of the Second World War encouraged a more liberal attitude towards equities. Common stocks have provided a gradually increasing proportion of their investment portfolio.

At the end of 1963, institutions held about 20 per cent of the common stock listed on the New York Stock Exchange, compared with 12·7 per cent in 1949. If these trends continue they will hold about 24 per cent in 1970 and 30 per cent in 1980. (Institutions already hold about 80 per cent of corporate bonds.) Inevitably the emergence of the large institutional investors has had an important effect on relationships between management and shareholder.

The institutions are sophisticated investors, demanding very detailed information about a company's activities before deciding whether or not to buy its shares. Their representatives make frequent visits to the company; while they are mainly concerned with eliciting information, their comments on company policies or proposed new ventures may be influential. An organization like the Massachusetts Investors Trust contains specialists in particular industries whose views carry considerable weight. They adopt a rational, professional approach to their investment decisions; it is partly due to their efforts that the business of investment analysis has come to acquire some of the characteristics of a 'science'. In New York and most other large cities there are societies of security analysts, and company chairmen frequently appear before them to report on their activities.

But the influence of the institutions on management should not be exaggerated. 'The business of stockholders is primarily to receive; the business of management is primarily to manage and create.'[5] Adolf Berle's dictum is still true of the institutional investors. Their concern is to make the best use of the money which has been entrusted to them. It is rare for them to hold more than 1 per cent of the stock of any one company, and they normally sell the stock if they become dissatisfied with its management. There have been cases where institutions have used their voting power to block a management proposal with which they disagreed – a new stock-option plan, for example, or a recapitalization scheme – and some commentators, worried by the 'irresponsibility' of management power, have urged the institutions to take a much more active part in the company's internal affairs. It is possible that the institutions will become bolder in influencing management decisions, but their main objective is to invest money in what they consider to be well-managed companies. Unlike the 'dominant shareholder' of the past, they have no ties to any one company, and, as soon as they lose confidence in its management, they will take their money elsewhere.

A less important but still significant restraint on management freedom comes from the so-called 'corporate democrats', private individuals who make it their business to ensure that the rights of stockholders are respected. One of the purposes of the Securities and Exchange Commission was to create the conditions for 'shareholder democracy', in which an active and informed body of shareholders would have a vote in the councils of every publicly owned company. As has been seen, the diffusion of share ownership and the apparent apathy of the typical shareholder have to some extent freed management from ownership control. But some companies have deliberately aggravated the problem by holding their annual meetings in remote towns, by providing only the minimum of information in their annual reports, and in general by taking a casual approach to shareholder relations.

In militant opposition to this trend are people like Lewis Gilbert, Mrs Wilma Soss (founder of the Federation of Women Shareholders in American Business), and others, who frequently attend annual meetings and insist that the rights of shareholders should be respected. Their questions are often embarrassing to management, but there is no doubt that they have focused public attention on questionable company policies.

Sidney Weinberg, a partner in a leading investment banking firm and a director of many companies, recently accused the 'corporate democrats' of turning the stockholders' meeting into a circus. He urged company chairmen to be more ruthless in ruling 'impertinent' questions out of order and to curb publicity-seekers by eliminating stockholder identification from reports of annual meetings. In this speech, which was made shortly after a particularly unruly meeting of stockholders in the Communications Satellite Corporation, Weinberg defended the right of stockholders to ask management 'pertinent, sensible, constructive questions', but suggested that questions about the company's day-to-day operations, or from shareholders representing special interest groups (such as organized labour, or the Negro community) were improper.

Many company directors enthusiastically applauded Weinberg's comments and they have taken steps to squash 'impertinence' by shareholders at annual meetings. But some businessmen are uneasy. While it is agreed that the circus atmosphere (which some firms have stimulated by providing lavish free lunches, entertainment, and displays of products) is to be avoided, there is some doubt over the right of management to define whether questions are pertinent or impertinent. It seems unreasonable to confine shareholders' questions to the firm's financial results. If the shareholders cannot ask questions about the company's attitude, say, to the hiring of Negroes, who else can? Submissive shareholders make life easier for management, but they also remove an important check on managerial freedom of action.

The activities of the corporate democrats have given new life to the annual meeting; by their aggressive attitude towards management they have performed a useful service to other investors. Both the professional scrutiny of the institutional investors and the cruder attacks by the 'C.D.s' have forced companies to improve their disclosure standards and made them more accountable to the public as a whole.

This is not meant to suggest that shareholder democracy is feasible in any literal sense or that the spread of the share-owning habit will 'democratize' American industry or create a 'people's capitalism'. The latter is the slogan used by the New York Stock Exchange as part of its unceasing campaign to encourage more people to own shares. Keith Funston, president of the Exchange, has spoken of raising the number of shareholders from 20 million to 50 million over the next twenty-five years, and there is a strong ideological strain in his promotional addresses.

The American system of widespread shareownership [he has said] is generally regarded today as a major contribution to the philosophy and successful practice of capitalism in the United States. To the entire Free World wide shareownership has come to symbolize a form of American industrial democracy worthy of emulation.

The Exchange has tried to foster the share-owning habit among lower-income groups through investment clubs and such devices as the Monthly Investment Plan, which, started in 1954, enables people to invest in stocks on a budget of as little as $40 every three months.

Investment in equities is riskier than most other forms of saving, since the value of the investment may decline, but it offers the possibility of large capital gains if the market price goes up. The stock market is a vehicle partly for saving, partly for gambling. The gambling element can sometimes get out of hand, as it did in 1959-61, when the shares in many speculative companies were pushed to unrealistic heights, paving the way for the dramatic market collapse in 1962. Because of the risks involved, it can be argued that share ownership below certain income levels should not be encouraged. At present stock ownership, despite Funston's efforts, is still highly concentrated in the wealthiest sections of the population. The richest one per cent of the population probably holds at least two thirds of all the corporate stock outstanding.[6]

A more equal distribution of this form of wealth may be desirable on social grounds, but the recruitment of low-income investors has not proved easy. The Monthly Investment Plan has not proved profitable for most of the brokerage houses which have undertaken it, with the exception of Wall Street's largest broker, Merrill Lynch Pierce Fenner & Smith, which is responsible for 60 per cent of the 125,000 M.I.P. accounts now outstanding. Moreover, there is not much likelihood that an increase in the number of shareholders will make a significant difference to the way large corporations are managed. The typical investor is interested in making money for himself, but he has no tie to any one corporation, and no incentive to concern himself with its management, except in so far as his own limited interests are concerned.

Of all those standing in relation to the large corporation [it has been said], the shareholder is least subject to its power. Through the mechanism of the security markets, his relationship to the corporation is rendered highly abstract and formal, quite limited in scope, and readily reducible to monetary terms. . . . Shareholder democracy, so-called, is misconceived because the shareholders are not the governed of the corporation whose consent must be sought. If they are, it is only in the most limited sense. Their interests are protected if financial information is made available, fraud and overreaching are prevented, and a market is maintained in which their shares may be sold.[7]

Sources of Funds

If the shareholders have little influence on company management, is the stock market itself, often regarded as the 'nub' of the capitalist system, an institution of little significance? The traditional function of the stock market was to channel the savings of individuals to businesses and corporations which needed money. But the most important source of capital for the corporation comes from the customer who buys its products. Internal sources, retained profits and depreciation allowances, typically account for about 60 per cent of the corporation's funds, and in many cases the proportion is higher. The gap is filled by borrowing from the banks or by raising money 'in the market'. The latter may take the form of bond issues or of stock issues. The bond issues may be sold either publicly, in the bond market, or privately, when the borrowing corporation negotiates directly with the lender. In either case institutional investors, the insurance companies and pension funds in particular, are the principal lenders; individual investors play very small part in the corporate bond market.

Stock or equity issues appear to be declining in importance as a source of finance for corporations. In recent years there has been a steady inflow of funds into the stock market from institutions, far exceeding the supply of new equity issues. Hence the institutions have had to purchase stock from existing holders, principally individuals. Sidney Homer, a partner in Salomon Brothers and Hutzler, has pointed out that between 1959 and 1963 the institutions put an average of $2,600 million a year into the equity market and foreigners put in $200 million. These combined purchases exceeded the net volume of new stocks created (which amounted to $1,500 million) so that other investors, mostly individuals, were net liquidators of $1,300 million a year. The stock market, says Homer, has increasingly become a scarcity market.[8]

In the decade from 1954 to 1963 net new security issues (both equity and debt) declined from 26·3 per cent of total corporate sources of funds to only 11·6 per cent. There has been a steady surge in retained earnings and depreciation. To the extent that external financing was required, it was mostly handled through borrowing rather than sale of new common shares. Equity capital is regarded as the costliest kind of capital to raise, since interest payments on debt are tax deductible, and dividend payments on stock are not.

In 1963 American companies repurchased more stock than they issued. They bought their own stock for a variety of reasons – to 'retire' it and so reduce the number of shares outstanding, or to use it for rewarding their executives in stock-option schemes, or to use it in acquiring other companies through an exchange of shares. These stock repurchase programmes, which appear to be growing, have aroused considerable controversy. (The practice is unknown and illegal in Britain.) While it may be a useful device enabling some companies to rationalize their capital structure, it is regarded by some critics as an admission of failure, indicating that the managers cannot find profitable outlets for their surplus cash. The money, these critics argue, belongs to the shareholders and should be returned to them in the form of higher dividends.

The only consistent source of new equity issues on a large scale has been the utilities, especially American Telephone and Telegraph, whose ability to generate internal funds is limited by Government control of rates. But the supply of new issues from this source has not prevented a situation of scarcity in the stock market; this is one of the factors responsible for the underlying rise in stock prices.

If these trends continue, it seems that the prime function of the stock market is to provide a means whereby the ownership of wealth is shifted from one hand to another. Naturally companies will still use the stock market to raise money, and the process of privately owned companies deciding to 'go public' will continue. But it is worth noting that some of the reasons for 'going public' are hardly in line with the traditional view of the stock market's role. Thus when Foote, Cone & Belding, a leading advertising agency, sold shares to the public for the first time, the main reasons for doing so were, first, that the company was required under its previous rules to buy back all the shares held by the officers when they retired; it was better to allow the public to buy the shares than for the company to buy them out of its own reserves. Second, 'it seemed to be in the interest of all the shareholders for tax and other reasons to have a publicly established value for the stock.' Third, it enabled the company to recruit executives with the help of stock-option schemes. Finally, a public valuation of the stock would be helpful in acquiring other companies.[9]

The decline of equity issues and the growing importance of 'private placements' with institutional investors have had the incidental effect of lessening the significance of the investment banking firms which in the early years of the century played a dominant role in American industry. In those days they were both investment and commercial bankers, but the Banking Act of 1934 separated the two activities; they were forced to choose one or the other. The leading underwriting companies like Morgan Stanley, Kuhn Loeb, and Dillon Read are represented on the boards of directors of many companies, but often they are more concerned with advising the company treasurer how to invest his surplus cash than with finding new sources of finance. Some of these investment banking firms have substantial resources of their own, and they can play a genuinely 'capitalistic' role in seeking out speculative opportunities and risking their own money. This may involve backing an unknown company, as Lehman did with Litton Industries and Kuhn Loeb with Polaroid, or it may mean the purchase of an ailing company (like Avis, the car rental company, which was bought by Lazard Frères), its reorganization and subsequent sale at a higher price.

Attitudes to shareholders, and to the stock market in general, vary considerably between companies. Thus Wrigley, the chewing-gum firm, describes itself as 'more of a stockholder company than a professional management company',[10] and here dividends took precedence over growth. Between 1953 and 1962 after-tax earnings fluctuated between $10 million and $12 million, and no less than 83 per cent of the earnings were paid out in dividends. But in the larger and more diversified enterprises there is greater reliance on internal funds, and profits on one product may be used to finance losses on another. In General Electric, for example, the chairman once said, 'the older businesses have to pay for the new.' This does not involve a policy of deliberate cross-subsidization between products – each division of the group is expected to stand on its own feet; but General Electric's entry into the computer and nuclear power markets, involving several years of heavy losses before a break-even point was reached, would not have been possible without the consistent profits made on such older products as electric lamps.

In this case there appears to be no 'market test' for investment. It may be that the cost of external funds plays a part in the calculation which the company makes to determine where the investment should be made. But in some cases the investing company may be accepting a rate of return on investment which is lower than might be achieved by the shareholders if the surplus funds were returned to them to invest in other fields. In other cases the company may be aiming at too high a return on investment, and its funds may be kept idle for too long while opportunities for such a return are sought. In either case the decision is for the corporation executives to make, and it is not forced on them by the market.

Many large companies appear to have set for themselves certain target rates of return, both on new investments and on their total invested capital, to which their operations are geared over a long term. Return on investment is what counts. 'We look to the health of the business as being more important than growth – if one has to choose,' says the chairman of Du Pont. 'I would rather have a $3,000 million business at a 10 per cent [after-tax] return than a $6,000 million business at a 5 per cent return or even a 6 per cent return.' The profit rate which they aim to achieve may be arrived at on the basis of their past experience, the performance of rival companies, and perhaps the expectations of the financial community. It is misleading to say that they aim to 'maximize' profits, since they are inclined not to take advantage of short-term situations to achieve an above-average rate of return. The first concern of the manager is profit, but this is best considered as profit for the corporation, not for the shareholders nor for the manager himself. Both the manager and the shareholders benefit from high profits, but it is the corporation which is of primary importance.

Many companies try to keep an ample supply of ready cash in their treasuries, simply because they do not like to have to consult with lenders or with investment bankers every time they make a new investment. But when they do go to the market for funds, they are not necessarily sacrificing their independence. In contrast to the old state of affairs when the capitalist hired the manager, now it is the manager who hires the capitalist.

An efficient capital market, of course, is essential, but the business of buying and selling stocks is only one aspect of the capital market and not necessarily the most important part. The stockbrokers and investment houses are naturally eager that the business of buying and selling stocks should grow, and the increasing importance of institutional investors is disturbing for them, for the institutions are inclined to hold stock for the long term; the turnover rate on the New York Stock Exchange has been declining steadily for the past fifty years. Stock has a tendency to stay put. But the question of whether the number of 'small investors' should be greatly enlarged, as the New York Stock Exchange wants, is one that needs to be more carefully examined. The ability to raise money from the public as well as from institutions is an essential element in an efficient and flexible capital market. It is possible that industry's reliance on internally generated funds, which has aroused speculation that the United States may be becoming a capital-surplus economy, will be temporary. But there are risks involved in the unlimited extension of the share-owning habit among lower-income groups.

The stock market can be considered as a vehicle for savings, as a gambling centre, and as a barometer of public opinion. In its latter role the index of stock prices is usually included among lists of 'economic indicators', and there is a sense in which 'business confidence' may be influenced by the behaviour of the stock market. In the long run, obviously, the stock market will reflect the cyclical swings in the economy which in turn affect the profits of individual companies. If a company needs to raise money from the public, it may be forced to delay as long as more people are selling stocks than buying them. But the connexion between short-term fluctuations in the stock market and the investment decisions of corporations is often remote. The relatively insignificant economic consequences of the stock market collapse in 1962 suggest that, even as an economic indicator, Wall Street is not the power that once it was.

6 · The Conservative Unions

Management Takes the Offensive

THE businessman wants as much freedom as possible to manage his enterprise profitably and efficiently. The trade union, concerned with the security and well-being of its members, tries to impose limitations on the employer's freedom. Hence the formation of unions was fiercely resisted by management; it was only with the help of the Federal Government, through the favourable legislation of the New Deal, that collective bargaining between union and employer became firmly established in American industry. But faced with the existence of powerful unions and the need to negotiate with them, American businessmen have begun to apply to labour relations the same scientific, rational approach that they try to follow in marketing, finance, production, and the other functions of management.

The successful company works out for itself a labour relations policy, based on the need to maintain the profitability of the enterprise, preserve management's freedom to manage, and develop a stable relationship with the union. The policy will be implemented firmly and consistently. A company with good labour relations, measured not merely by the degree of industrial peace that prevails in its plants, but rather by the level of its production costs in relation to other firms in the same industry, generally has an edge over its competitors in other respects. Both labour-relations performance and financial performance depend principally on the quality of management. There is much wider recognition in the U.S. than in Britain that the productivity of labour depends on management, that progressive union attitudes go hand in hand with progressive management. There is very little evidence to suggest that British workers work less hard than American workers. Weak management may have allowed bad habits to take root (as has happened in some American industries), and these are often difficult to correct. But in so far as British labour relations are bad, the most important reason is probably poor management, reflected in amateurish or inconsistent labour relations policies. In the United States the handling of labour relations, like other aspects of management, has gradually become professionalized.

Some companies were far-sighted enough to adopt a consistent policy, and to stick to it, soon after collective bargaining was established. A more general response was defensive, with management reacting to aggressive union demands and settling for as few concessions as possible. During the Second World War, and the lush seller's market that followed, resistance to union demands was often feeble, since higher labour costs could usually be passed on to consumers in the form of higher prices. The competitive conditions that developed in the mid 1950s forced a change in attitude; management began to take the initiative, not simply by refusing to be bullied into over-generous concessions, but in formulating proposals of its own which would improve efficiency as well as satisfy union demands. Each proposal is based on detailed analysis of all relevant factors, including the desires and motivations of the employees. As one frustrated union leader put it:

They couldn't stop us on the picket line; they couldn't stop us by straight-arm tactics; and so they have been studying human relations in the economic, social and political fields to find out how to stop unions.[1]

The employers want the workers to be loyal to them, and, in consequence, 'all the things we fought for the corporation is now giving the workers'.

The rational approach to labour relations is by no means universal; and sometimes management's attempt to regain the initiative takes more traditional forms. The attitude of the Chrysler executive who described collective bargaining (in 1944) 'as an assault on liberty, as an evil thing which is against the public interest, as something which will increase poverty' is still sometimes found in the boardrooms of American industry. The history of labour relations in America has been bloody and violent, and the scars have not completely healed. Talk of 'rolling back' the unions is still heard. In the political sphere there is talk (but little action) about applying the antitrust laws to the unions, so that each union could represent only the employees of a single employer, or perhaps even a single plant. There is a reluctance on the part of some employers to accept unions as an integral part of the business system. The allegedly excessive power of unions continues to be a live political issue.

But for most employers the recurrent attempts to weaken the power of unions by political action are of limited interest. They have found that most of their objectives can be fulfilled at the bargaining table. A firm labour relations policy, moreover, does not necessarily involve anti-union attitudes; it is based on the frank recognition that the interests of the two sides are different and sometimes conflicting, but that collective bargaining provides a means whereby the differences may be resolved. A self-consciously pro-union attitude is often a cloak for lax discipline and over-manning – in short, for bad management. The contrast in this respect between Studebaker, which was widely admired for its 'constructive' approach to labour relations, and General Motors, usually regarded as tough and inflexible, is instructive. The former (which abandoned car production in the U.S. in 1964) not only paid higher wages than the rest of the industry for most of the postwar period, but its production standards were inferior, its manning was excessive, its rest periods too long, and its enforcement of contract provisions generally weak. General Motors, on the other hand, had always maintained tight production standards (even during the period of booming demand when the competitive spur to efficiency was absent) and has insisted on its right to deploy its manpower efficiently and to discipline employees who violate the contract. At the same time, there is no evidence that worker dissatisfaction is greater in General Motors' plants than elsewhere in the industry, and its strike record is probably better than that of its rivals. While the superior financial resources of General Motors may have enabled it to stand up to the union more aggressively than Studebaker, it was bad management, not financial weakness, which underlay Studebaker's abnormally high labour costs.[2]

The example of General Motors is now being followed by other companies which, like Studebaker, allowed their employment practices to deteriorate during the early postwar period. They are trying to be tougher and more sophisticated. Although the larger unions have tried to match the companies by devoting more resources to research and training – and they are certainly far better equipped in this respect than most British unions – management negotiators are often more skilful and better prepared than their union antagonists. This is a marked contrast from the situation that prevailed ten or fifteen years ago.

An extreme example of the new management approach is 'Boulwarism', developed by General Electric under the direction of its vice-president in charge of labour relations, Lemuel Boulware. A long strike in 1946 forced the company to reappraise its labour relations policy, and, under Boulware's guidance, it began to apply the tools of marketing to the problem – market research, product planning, market development, and merchandising.

Instead of offering less than it intends to give, then permitting the union to force (or often appear to force) it to grant more, General Electric, after its careful research, puts what it believes is proper on the table and changes this only on the basis of what it considers new information.[3]

The company's research includes an analysis of union demands, but the main purpose is to avoid 'haggling'. Once the company's offer is formulated, it is 'sold' to the employees by means of an extensive advertising and public relations campaign.

Despite the violent opposition of Mr James Carey, the leader of the International Union of Electrical Workers, the company had some success with its new technique, notably in 1960, when an attempted strike against the company's offer was defeated by widespread back-to-work movements among the rank-and-file union members. But the union appealed to the National Labour Relations Board; this is the government agency which was created in 1935 to uphold the rights of employees and the duties of employers in collective bargaining. In 1964 the Board ruled that the company was guilty of an unfair labour practice. According to the Board, General Electric had failed to recognize that collective bargaining was 'a shared process in which each party had the right to play an active role' and that the law required an employer 'to deal with the employees through the union, not with the union through the employees'. In refusing to budge from its initial offer, said the Board, the company was reducing collective bargaining to a mere formality.

General Electric will appeal against the Board's ruling to the Supreme Court, but, whatever the Court's decision, it is unlikely that Boulware's approach to labour relations will be widely imitated. It does, nevertheless, reflect a widespread feeling among American businessmen that management should stand up for its rights, should not only fight for a 'reasonable' contract, but should ensure that the provisions of the contract are enforced. The more sophisticated managements will try hard to avoid a major trial of strength with the union, but when a genuine issue of principle is involved, as in the steel negotiations of 1959, there is perhaps a greater willingness than in the past to take a long strike. The desire to be tough is usually tempered by a clearer understanding of the pressures to which the union bargainers are subject, and, in most cases, by sympathy with the union's objectives. There is not much evidence that industrial unrest has been aggravated by the new management militancy; as measured by the decline in the number and duration of strikes, especially since 1960, labour–management relations are much more peaceful than they were in the early postwar years.

The Unions Lose Their Élan

In seeking to eliminate restrictive practices and to improve industrial efficiency, American businessmen are assisted by several factors. First and most important is the permissive attitude on the part of the American worker and the American union towards management efficiency. The American union

seeks security for itself through the closed or union shop and for the worker through the seniority clause and the grievance machinery. It then allows the employer to run the enterprise within the limits set by these provisions for institutional and personal security and also by competition in the product market.[4]

The absence of ideology in the American labour movement, which reflects the individualism and mobility of American society, has kept the United States free of the divisive class conflict that has been a serious obstacle to industrial peace and to economic progress in other countries. There are, of course, many British companies which have succeeded in establishing the right to manage and which have enjoyed both a steady rise in labour productivity and a stable relationship with the unions. But it is probable that the persistence of class conflict in Britain and the anti-capitalist bias of many unions have been handicaps. (It appears, too, that while American unions are generally aggressive in seeking new gains for their members, British unions tend to be more defensive in trying to conserve their existing position, though this may simply reflect cautious attitudes on the part of management.) In the United States there is little inclination to 'change the system', since most people, both employer and employee, seem to benefit from it; as long as the managers are efficient, the union is generally happy to let them get on with the job. This does not prevent conflict over the impact of particular management decisions on the well-being of the employees; but the basic principle of the manager's right to manage is accepted.

Second, just as excess capacity and severe competition have led to a tougher management line on labour costs, so high unemployment in the 1955–65 period has weakened the unions' bargaining power. Most of the unions in the mass-production industries have lost members in recent years, partly because of slack demand for their employers' products, partly because technological change has reduced manpower requirements.

Third, the labour movement itself appears to have lost its old *élan*.

Little is left of the proselytizing spirit that created the basic organizations in the building and printing trades in the late nineteenth and early twentieth centuries, the needle trades organizations in the following two decades, and the industrial unions in the thirties.[5]

After its spectacular growth between 1930 and 1945, when union membership rose from 3 million to 12 million, from 12 per cent of the labour force to 36 per cent, membership rose much more

TABLE 4

Union membership 1930–62
(in millions)

1930	3·16
1935	3·61
1940	7·06
1945	12·01
1950	14·01
1955	16·04
1960	15·54
1962	14·88

slowly to just over 16 million in the mid 1950s; by 1962 the figure had dropped to below 15 million. The growth of union membership in Britain also slowed down in the postwar period, but only after a much larger proportion of the labour force had been unionized. Mass unionism in the U.S.A. has been largely dependent on production workers in manufacturing industry, and this is the area where employment has grown least. Although white-collar employment exceeded blue-collar employment for the first time in 1956, the labour movement has found it difficult to evolve an organizing strategy that offers much prospect of significant gains in the white-collar trades. Only 13 per cent of all union members are white-collar workers – a mere 2·3 million out of a possible total of 22 million – compared with over 20 per cent in Britain. Some progress has been made among government employees and among teachers, but the huge and growing number of workers in retail and wholesale trade, in finance and insurance and most of the service trades are relatively unorganized, and at least one much-trumpeted success among professional workers – Engineers and Scientists of America – has collapsed.

It is possible that the impact of changing technology on white-collar workers, notably the introduction of computers, will create feelings of insecurity and make the need for union organization more obvious. But management is likely to resist such a development, and its resistance will be a good deal more sophisticated and effective than it was when industrial unions were being formed in the 1930s. It is questionable, too, whether the labour movement has either the organizational structure or the enthusiasm necessary for a full-scale organizing drive. The centre of the movement, the American Federation of Labour–Congress of Industrial Organizations, is not much more than a federation of largely autonomous unions. The merger of the two bodies in 1957 – the older A.F.L. had pioneered the creation of craft unions,

TABLE 5

Membership of ten largest unions 1962

Teamsters	1,457,252
Automobile	1,073,547
Steel	878,516
Machinists	867,759
Electrical	793,000
Carpenters	739,207
Mine	450,000
Hotel	445,000
Ladies' Garment	441,000
Hod Carriers	429,279

while the C.I.O. had broken away in the 1930s to form the industrial unions – did not produce the accession of strength that had been hoped for. The new body did something to reduce jurisdictional disputes between unions and to discourage the 'raiding' of another union's members, but there were still too many industries served by competing unions, and the A.F.L.–C.I.O. was unable to persuade them to merge. The A.F.L.–C.I.O. also tried to enforce ethical rules of conduct on its member unions; the expulsion of the country's largest union, the International Brotherhood of Teamsters (which represents mostly truck drivers), in 1957 was a dramatic use of centralized power. But it was soon apparent that the union had lost little as a result of the expulsion. It retained the support of its members, and its assistance continued to be sought in industrial disputes by unions affiliated to the A.F.L.–C.I.O.

Attempts by the unions to enlarge their influence have been handicapped, too, by the unfavourable image of the labour movement in the mind of the public. This is partly due to the revelations of racketeering and corruption in the labour movement during the Congressional hearings on improper activities in the labour–management field, held under the chairmanship of Senator McClellan between 1956 and 1958. Although racketeering has generally been limited to industries that contain a multiplicity of small employers, and although the most notorious unions like the Teamsters, the International Longshoremen's Association and the Bakery and Confectionery Workers were all expelled from the A.F.L.–C.I.O. after their practices had been exposed, there is still a widespread impression that some union leaders possess considerable power which they tend to use irresponsibly. This impression is confirmed by the apparent absence of democracy in some unions; the president, once installed, remains in the office until he dies, and his attitude to the rank and file is often high-handed. That democracy is not impossible in the trade unions is shown by the example of the International Typographers Union, where a fully developed two-party system of government is in operation, though it is doubtful whether this contributes to constructive labour–management relations; the union has bitterly opposed the introduction of automation in printing. The United Auto Workers, under the guidance of Walter Reuther, has tried to foster democratic procedures; its Public Review Board, an independent agency formed in 1957 and consisting of seven members drawn from the public, enables rank-and-file members to appeal against decisions of the union leadership and, if the Board accepts the appeal, to get them reversed.[6] Recent contested elections in the steel, coalmining and electrical unions suggest that presidential offices are not always as safe as they seem. In these larger unions there are signs of greater restlessness among rank-and-file members, especially on local issues which, they feel, are ignored or neglected by the union bosses.

Another difficulty is the inability of the labour movement to retain the support of the liberals and idealists who had been an important source of strength in the days when unions were struggling for recognition. In the 1930s the formation of unions, like the Republican side in the Spanish Civil War, was a cause worth fighting for. In the 1960s, the civil rights movement has taken its place. To young idealists filled with revolutionary fervour the unions appear to be too complacent and too willing to cooperate with the employers instead of battling against them. The liberals outside the unions (including some frustrated socialists) tend to denounce the labour movement for its sterility and lack of idealism. Within the movement, too, there are signs of frustration.

What are we here for? [asked one leader]: to maintain a docile labor force by seeing that people get enough in the way of wages and fringe benefits and finally go to the grave well fed and content? Life consists of more than that.[7]

But his only suggestion for action was that the unions should adopt a more aggressively independent political role. Certainly the political achievements of the labour movement have been meagre in the past decade; it has generally supported the social-welfare measures of the Democrats, and its support has been very valuable, but it has shown little originality or social initiative. Walter Reuther has spoken of turning the unions into a social movement, 'a conscious, articulate social force, one that de-emphasizes the purely material things and deals with those broad social and philosophical values which determine the quality of our society'. But there is not much evidence that the rank and file of the unions want such a movement.

The fact is that the labour movement as it has developed has deliberately posed for itself limited objectives and has steered clear of political involvement, except in so far as the rights of unions are threatened. Union men complain about the 'total capture of society by the corporate structure', but the labour movement itself has been unable to envisage, much less try to create, any society other than one in which the business corporation was dominant. While there has been a small anti-capitalist element in the movement, it has never had a significant influence. The unions have given their assent to the existing social and economic framework, and have not tried to alter it except in minor ways. 'It is probable', one writer suggests, 'that never before has there existed a labour movement which has voluntarily so well integrated itself with its society'.[8] The labour movement has been a force for conservatism, contributing to the stability of American society. This does not mean that the unions have not been effective and imaginative in the pursuit of their limited objectives – much more so, probably, than British unions. The presence in the movement of men like Reuther, who is not only a passionate champion of human rights (he was the only union leader who threw his full support behind the Negroes' march on Washington in 1963), but an aggressive innovator in labour–management relations, will help to prevent the unions from sinking into lethargy. His union, the United Auto Workers, keeps the motor-industry management constantly on its guard, in the political arena as well as at the bargaining table. One of its recent moves was to open a campaign against the evils of 'monopsony' or monopoly buying power. The giant motor companies, the union argues, use their buying power to drive too hard a bargain with the component suppliers; these firms, with their profit margins squeezed to the limit, are unable to afford adequate wages and pension benefits for their employees, who are, of course, members of the U.A.W. There is probably enough sympathy for this argument in Washington to merit an investigation of the issue by one of the Congressional Committees; even if no legislation results, the campaign might well have some effect on relations between the motor manufacturers and their component suppliers.

But this kind of tactic does not amount to a serious challenge to the system as a whole, or even to the distribution of power within the system. If the structure or quality of American society is ever to be changed in any radical way, it is highly unlikely that the unions will be responsible for it.

Collective Bargaining

The conservatism of the unions does not mean that their role in society is unimportant, or that their influence on management is negligible. They have played a vital role in safeguarding employees against unilateral and arbitrary actions by management. Through the institution of collective bargaining, they have forced employers to pay close and continuous attention to personnel relations, and to weigh carefully the consequence of proposed actions, such as the introduction of new methods and new machinery, on their employees.

Perhaps the most important achievement of collective bargaining in the United States is

the creation of a system of industrial jurisprudence, a system under which employer and employee rights are set forth in contractual form and disputes over the meaning of the contract are settled through a rational grievance process usually ending, in the case of unresolved disputes, in arbitration.[9]

Collective bargaining is only thirty years old in most industries, but the principle of legally binding contracts, usually lasting for two years or more, is firmly established.

One consequence is that there are far fewer 'wildcat' or unofficial strikes than in Britain, because the participants can be dismissed or otherwise disciplined by the management. Unofficial strikes in violation of the contract still occur, of course, but they represent a serious problem only to those companies whose management lacks the determination to discipline the offenders. If the management is firm, the union leaders are better able to keep their members under control. If the management pursues vacillating policies, the authority of the union leaders is undermined. It has been argued that Britain's unofficial strike problem will only be overcome if the American system of legally binding contracts is adopted; but it is possible that a large part of the answer lies in the attitudes of management.

In the United States most strikes occur over the negotiation of a new contract to replace one that has expired. This has the advantage of permitting the company, the union, and the company's suppliers and customers, to prepare for a possible strike at a fixed point in time, but the disadvantage is that the key issues tend to be left until just before the old contract is due to expire. The negotiations take place in an atmosphere of crisis which does not encourage constructive discussion. The number of strikes has, in fact, been declining, especially since 1960, but there have been several long and serious strikes, such as the 116-day steel strike in 1959 and the 114-day New York newspaper strike in 1963. To a large extent these strikes have stemmed from the clash between the union's desire for job security in a period of high unemployment and rapid technological change and the employer's drive for efficiency, often involving the removal of restrictive practices that had been allowed to creep in during the earlier period.

As in most other industrialized countries, public impatience with strikes has been rising, and this may account for the increased willingness of the Federal Government to intervene in collective bargaining negotiations that have either reached deadlock or seem likely to do so. The Taft–Hartley Act of 1947 gives the President the power to act in the case of emergency disputes, and the powers have been used a score of times in various industries, principally the docks. There is also a well-established Federal Mediation and Conciliation Service, which has played an important behind-the-scenes role in suggesting new approaches to labour–management problems and in improving the flexibility of collective bargaining. But the recent tendency has been for almost any serious dispute to be regarded as a national emergency and for the Secretary of Labour, and sometimes the President himself, to take an active part in solving it. This runs the risk of removing from the parties concerned the onus of settling their differences by themselves. It may be that the interminable labour disputes on the railways and in the docks have been aggravated by the knowledge on both sides that the Federal Government would almost certainly step in to prevent a strike. The importance of the long-strike option (short strikes are becoming less common and less significant as collective bargaining becomes more sophisticated) is that it creates strong pressures towards agreement, and that, when a long strike occurs, it usually (though not always) has beneficial results on future bargaining relationships.

Thus the 1959 steel strike was followed by the creation of a joint labour–management Human Relations Committee to provide for the continuous study of mutual problems without the pressure of contract expiry dates, midnight deadlines, and the familiar atmosphere of crisis. The committee's work does not replace the formal negotiations that take place when a new contract is being worked out, but it is concerned with fact-finding, the identification and clarification of problems, and research into possible solutions for these problems. Such continuous bargaining had been used previously in other industries, but its use in the steel industry, and its apparent success in paving the way for peaceful settlements in 1962 and 1963 have led to its imitation by others, notably the New York newspaper industry and the motor industry. As Walter Reuther describes it,

these study committees are not bargaining; their purpose is to try to assemble all the basic information so that when bargaining time comes, the facts will be known to both sides and decisions can be based upon these and not upon the economic power that each of us can muster.

The use of private power, by union and by employer, must be accepted as legitimate if collective bargaining is to survive, but there are indications that the power is being used more cautiously, and that the rational, problem-solving aspect of collective bargaining is being enlarged.

There are some problem areas where collective bargaining is working badly. In the railway industry, in shipping and the docks, in the airline industry, the fragmentation of the unions, the uncertainties of government policy, and the inconsistency of the employers have combined to create a highly unstable situation in which strikes are common and cooperative approaches to problems are rare. It is notable that labour relations in the road-haulage industry, despite the racketeering and corruption associated with the Teamsters and their leader, James Hoffa, have generally been stable. In 1964 this union succeeded in negotiating its first industry-wide contract with the road-haulage industry represented by Trucking Employers Inc., an association of some 16,000 firms. While there are fears that the agreement gives the union the potential power to cripple a key segment of the nation's economy, it may well be better to have a single union in this position than the multiplicity of unions that compete against each other in the other transport industries.

Collective bargaining has become more complex, partly because the objectives of the parties have changed. The unions, after fighting first for recognition, then for higher wages, then for fringe benefits like health insurance, pensions, and supplementary unemployment payments, have turned their attention to job security in the face of technological change. The employers, instead of reacting defensively to union demands, are being forced by economic pressures to make their own demands for changes in working conditions so as to achieve greater efficiency. While there are some cases of outright union resistance to technological change, the most usual union response has been willing acceptance; the dockers on the East Coast have resisted containerization, the International Typographers Union has resisted the introduction of automatic typesetters, but most of the industrial unions have accepted change in return for the higher benefits that improved efficiency would bring to their members.

In some cases the union has actively fostered the introduction of new machinery; the United Mine Workers, under John L. Lewis, played a positive role in improving the productivity of the coalmining industry and its efforts, besides helping to phase the introduction of new machinery in a way that would be least painful to its members, are partly responsible for the highly competitive price of coal in relation to other fuels. A prosperous industry with a declining but increasingly well paid labour force was preferred to a vain fight for job stability. It is significant that this union has begun to adopt a somewhat different attitude in the last few years, principally because of high unemployment in the rest of the economy. As long as displaced miners could easily find jobs, the contraction of the industry's labour force posed few problems. But the lack of jobs forced many displaced miners, in desperate need of employment and wages, to accept work with non-union coalmine operators, who paid much lower wages than the unionized mines. The growth of non-union coal has threatened to undermine the U.M.W.'s traditional policy of encouraging mechanization in return for high wages and generous pensions. Competition from the small mine-owners, who did not pay these high wages and pensions, created difficulties for the unionized operators, and they, in turn, tried to keep their wage costs down.

The U.M.W.'s dilemma is aggravated by the fact that most of the displacement has occurred in the depressed Appalachian region; there are few other job opportunities here and yet the inhabitants are reluctant to move from their home communities. The experience of the last few years has shown that a union's willingness to accept technological change is likely to diminish as long as high unemployment persists.

There has been, nevertheless, some remarkable progress in tackling problems of technological change, even in industries where labour relations had been poor. The dockers on the West Coast, for example, after a series of violent strikes between 1934 and 1948, gradually moved away from their traditional policy of guerrilla resistance to management demands. In 1960 they signed a revolutionary agreement, giving management the right to introduce new methods of cargo handling in return for a $25 million pension and benefit fund to be financed by the employers over the $5\frac{1}{2}$-year life of the contract. Here was a case where, given an understanding by both sides of where their mutual interests lay, restrictive practices could be bought out. A crucial role was played by the union in educating its members and showing them what positive benefits they could obtain in return for accepting changes in long-established working conditions.

More imaginative is Kaiser Steel's Long Range Sharing Plan, which was adopted in 1963. The plan has two objectives. First, it is designed to relate earnings to productivity through an incentive scheme which would be more logical and more intelligible than traditional bonus schemes. The company agreed to share with its employees the benefits derived from cost savings in those areas of the company's activity where the savings could be directly attributed to the performance and attitudes of the hourly employees. Monthly bonuses were paid to the employees, varying in size according to the savings that were achieved in that month. After the first year a company official reported:

INDUSTRY IN THE U.S.A.

Beginnings of a new atmosphere in labor–management relations are apparent. Plant management can now approach problems of work practices previously considered too hot to handle in the face of violent opposition. Some supervisors, previously frustrated, now feel they are able to get their message to the workers and can motivate a successful response.

The second purpose of the plan was to find a constructive answer to the problem of job displacement arising from technological change. The company agreed that any employee displaced by new methods or new machinery would be guaranteed a place in the 'employment reserve pool', retained on the company's payroll, and assigned to any work which would not displace an employee elsewhere in the plant. The labour force would be reduced, but the reduction would be through the normal process of attrition, which at the Kaiser plant had been running at about 8 per cent of the work force each year.

Kaiser's plan was worked out jointly by the company and the union with the help of outside experts. The sharing aspect of the plan is not the same as the profit-sharing principle which is not uncommon in American industry. Interest in profit-sharing schemes was stimulated in 1961 when the United Auto Workers concluded such an agreement with American Motors, one of the smaller car manufacturers. This agreement, which was continued in the 1964–7 agreement, seemed to indicate an acceptance by the union of the need to relate wages at least partially to a firm's profitability. The union had in the past made special concessions to help a small firm stay in business. Although the U.A.W. has not so far extended the profit-sharing principle to the three giants of the industry, and is said to be not completely happy with the American Motors agreement, it is a possible step towards increasing cooperation between union and management.

Adjustments to technological change cannot always be handled through the normal process of attrition. In some collective bargaining agreements there is provision for 'severance pay', which for an experienced worker may amount to two or three times his annual earnings; this will enable him to finance a move to a different area or to cover the costs of retraining. A few firms, such as Armour, the meat-packing company, have gone further and made provision for a fund which would finance the retraining of workers likely to be displaced and the search for new job opportunities. Arrangements of this sort reflect the desire by unions and management to make long-term plans and to cushion the impact of technological change.

It is recognized, however, that the nation's need for adequate retraining facilities cannot be met solely through collective bargaining. Quite apart from its responsibility to maintain full employment, the Federal Government has been stepping up its retraining activities so as to facilitate the movement of workers in accordance with changes in industrial structure. There are obvious difficulties in transferring a worker from a declining manufacturing industry, where he may be earning $3·00 an hour, to service industries where the wage may only be $1·50 an hour; until the productivity of the service industries is increased, these gaps will persist and seriously inhibit labour mobility.

Some aspects of collective bargaining, moreover, tend to reduce labour mobility. Seniority rights often tie a worker to a particular plant or company, and, though some attempts have been made to develop seniority 'districts' on an industry-wide basis to facilitate job transfers, their coverage is still very limited. Secondly, pension rights are usually tied to length of service and reinforce the bond between worker and employer. Here again, there has been an increase in the 'vesting' of pension rights on behalf of employees, increasing the extent to which they can carry their rights with them when they leave for other employment. There have been proposals for the integration of private pension plans into the national social security system, so that pensions would be less directly tied to particular places of employment.

In the past five years there has been a significant shift of emphasis in Government manpower policy from the alleviation of unemployment towards more positive measures for increasing the adaptability of the labour force. Government-financed retraining programmes, for example, are supplementing the efforts being made by unions and management to cushion the effects of technological change. This does not mean that collective bargaining has lost its usefulness or has been made obsolete. On the contrary, there is considerable evidence to show that collective bargaining techniques are being adapted and refined to cope with unfamiliar problems; it is, indeed, a highly flourishing institution. Far from being replaced by Government manpower policies, it is the basis on which they rest.

Far less certain, however, is the relationship between collective bargaining and Government policies to curb inflation. In the United States, as in Britain, there have been periods when wages have risen faster than productivity, with the result that costs and prices have risen. The need for cost stability has been reinforced in the last few years by America's balance-of-payments problem; American manufacturers cannot hope to increase their share of the world's export markets if their costs and prices rise faster than those of their foreign competitors, as occurred, for example, in 1955-7. While there is much controversy over the extent to which unions have been responsible for inflation, it is agreed that powerful unions can use their power to negotiate wage increases which are in excess of the rise in productivity and so contribute to the pressure on costs.

As with the pricing power of large firms, the Government has attempted to bring pressure on unions to settle for 'non-inflationary' wage settlements. In 1961 the concept of 'guideposts' was introduced, providing a benchmark against which both price and wage increases could be judged. For the first few years after the guideposts were introduced, most major wage settlements satisfied the Administration's requirements. The guideposts certainly had some influence, but they were reinforced by the persistence of high unemployment and intense competition, which weakened the unions' bargaining power and stiffened the resistance of employers to large wage increases; there is an inverse relationship between the rate of unemployment and the average size of wage increases. But as the economy approaches full employment, the question of wage restraint is likely to assume a greater importance. In 1964, when unemployment was still high, the Johnson Administration was dismayed by the settlement in the motor industry which involved an increase in employment costs amounting to nearly 5 per cent. As unemployment continued to fall, the Administration became more concerned about inflationary wage increases in certain industries, notably construction. At the same time there were signs of increasing resentment among union leaders, who felt their members were entitled to larger wage increases than the guideposts permitted. The next few years will show whether the voluntary guidepost approach is sufficient, or whether the United States, like Britain, moves towards some more formal machinery for keeping wage movements under review.

7 · Reason in Management

New Systems of Control

THE crucial factor which determines the success or failure of an industrial enterprise is the quality of its management. Whether a firm manufactures cars or mines coal, whether it is in a growing or in a declining business, its chances of survival depend on the skill with which it is administered. The decline and eventual demise of Studebaker as an independent car maker stemmed from incompetent management, whose errors, aggravated by severe competition, could not be corrected. It is the depth of high-quality management in America's successful corporations which distinguishes them from their foreign counterparts. The United States is fortunate in that an unusually large proportion of the most talented individuals has been attracted to careers in industry, and, partly for this reason, the 'science' of management and industrial organization has been studied more intensively there than elsewhere.

Management involves the application of reason to complicated situations in which the consequences of a certain decision can rarely be predicted with complete accuracy. The successful manager needs both specialized knowledge and a highly developed faculty for weighing evidence and arriving at conclusions; the need for specialized knowledge is probably increasing as industry itself becomes more complex and as new techniques to aid the decision-making process are developed. Obviously, access to management posts must be based on competence, not on wealth or family connexions.

The qualities and qualifications needed for success in business have never been, and probably never will be, precisely defined, but the past fifty or sixty years have seen a steady advance in knowledge about the management of industry, which has helped to identify some of the factors that make for successful business performance. The accumulation of knowledge has not been systematized in a way that would make management, in the true

114

sense, a profession, but in a looser sense it has created a growing number of professional managers who are trained for the job. They owe no permanent allegiance to one company or one industry, and their talents can be applied to a wide range of problems and activities, in government as well as in business. Thus a man like Robert S. McNamara could apply what he called 'quantitative common sense' both to the problems of the Ford Motor Company (of which he was President) and to the problems of the U.S. Defence Department, of which he later became Secretary.

His administration of the Defence Department has been characterized by an absolute insistence on being systematic and rational. Instead of the jockeying and bargaining among interested parties that had often influenced the choice of weapons systems in the past, McNamara introduced new techniques of planning, programming and budgeting, which ensured that every major decision was based on a thorough analysis of all the alternatives. Under the influence of McNamara and the men who served under him, this ruthlessly analytical approach to management is spreading to other Government departments.

The transition from the intuitive, 'seat-of-the-pants' management of the past to the rational, sophisticated management approach which many companies now try to follow began towards the end of the last century. The size of industrial enterprises, especially the railways, was increasing to a point where new concepts of administration were needed. As growing companies like Swift, the meat-packing firm, extended their operations to encompass buying the raw material, manufacturing the finished product, and distributing it to consumers, it became necessary to separate out different managerial functions. The distinction between 'line' and 'staff' was evolved, the first steps were taken in cost accounting and stock control, and nation-wide advertising campaigns made their appearance. Frederick Taylor (1856–1915), the pioneer in 'scientific management', worked out methods of increasing the productivity of labour through better combinations of men and machines. By demonstrating in a practical manner how manufacturing processes could be rationally analysed and improved, he gave impetus to the idea that business itself could be studied in the same manner.

Taylor's work was mainly concerned with increasing the efficiency of a single process or a single plant. A little later the administration of a multi-plant corporation was analysed and refined. In the 1920s Alfred Sloan and his colleagues at General Motors evolved a new form of organization which combined the advantages of decentralization with effective coordinated control from the centre. Under the influence of William Durant, a creative genius but a casual administrator, General Motors had grown rapidly and haphazardly in the early years of the century, but ran into a severe financial crisis after the end of the First World War. It was rescued, partly by financial and management assistance from Du Pont, partly by Sloan's success in devising an organizational structure which has never been altered in any fundamental way and which has enabled the company to become the world's largest, and perhaps the most efficient, industrial enterprise. Sloan's plan 'distinguished policy from administration of policy, and specified the location of each in the structure'.[1] The company was divided into divisions, and an executive was placed in charge of each division with clearly defined responsibilities and clearly defined relationships to the central policy-making headquarters.

At the same time, an elaborate system of financial and statistical controls was developed which enabled the policy-makers at the centre to keep a careful and continuous check on the effectiveness of each division. The concept of 'standard volume' was used to work out a definite, long-term return-on-investment objective. As Sloan put it:

By applying a yardstick, unaffected by short-term volume fluctuations, we could isolate the extent to which we were deviating from our long-term profit goal and make a thorough evaluation of the underlying causes.[2]

The operating executives who ran the divisions had less freedom than they had before, under Durant's looser organization, but their responsibilities were more sharply defined, so that they could be held accountable for the performance of their divisions.

A somewhat similar organizational structure was adopted at about the same time by Du Pont. Difficulties in this company had arisen, not from excessive decentralization and inadequate control from head office, but from too much control; 'centralization' had been appropriate before the First World War, when the firm was almost entirely a manufacturer of explosives, but after the war, when the explosives business contracted sharply, a major diversification programme in other branches of the chemical industry was undertaken, and a different organization was required. A unique feature of Du Pont's system, initiated in 1921 under the presidency of Irénée du Pont, was its reliance on committee management. The executive committee consists of the president of the company and nine vice-presidents, who have no day-to-day functional responsibilities but who devote their full time to the company's activities as a whole. Each member of the committee, including the president, has one vote. The committee meets every week in the 'chart room', where the performance of each division is reviewed with its general manager. As in General Motors, the general manager of the division has considerable authority of his own – he is responsible for sales amounting to several hundred millions of dollars a year – and he is judged on the basis of how his division's return on investment compares with the objectives that have been set by the executive committee.[3]

The remarkable aspect of these two organizational reforms is that they have lasted. The success of the two companies was not dependent on one man – in this respect, as in many others, Sloan at General Motors was a complete contrast with Henry Ford at Ford – but on an approach to management which was apparently self-perpetuating. Other companies which have tried to adopt the General Motors or the Du Pont form of decentralization have often been unsuccessful. This suggests that the key to their success was not so much the specific structures that were adopted, but the management attitudes that underlay them. 'An essential aspect of our business philosophy', said Sloan, 'is the factual approach to business judgement'. It was the determination to get at the facts, to analyse them fully and objectively, and to take decisions only on the basis of such an analysis, which distinguished these two companies from their 'intuitive' rivals. 'General Motors', Sloan says, 'is not the appropriate organization for purely intuitive executives, but it provides a favourable environment for capable and rational men'.[4] The company may never produce an extraordinary genius like Henry Ford, and this in a sense is a weakness, but a comparison of the performance of General Motors with that of Ford Motor Company during the past thirty years leaves little doubt as to the superiority of the rational over the intuitive approach.

The Business Schools

While businessmen like Sloan were beginning to develop a scientific approach to management problems, business itself was gradually becoming established as a subject worthy of study at academic institutions. Prompted initially by the interest of economists in business problems, several universities created graduate schools of business administration around the turn of the century. The first was the Wharton School of Finance and Commerce, established at the University of Pennsylvania in 1881. Harvard's decision to substitute a business school for the school of diplomacy and government service that had first been planned reflects the inferior prestige of professions which in other countries have drained talent away from private industry. The Harvard Business School, it has been said,

was founded on a pioneering idea, simple and yet of astonishing potency, namely, that the administration of business enterprises needed to be and could be a professional matter worthy of the time and attention of learned, thoughtful, and responsible men.[5]

In 1920 there were business schools at nearly fifty universities, and by 1955 the number had more than tripled. At the start their academic status was low, and they were preoccupied with practical skills like book-keeping and accountancy. It was at Harvard in the 1920s that the study of business from a broad managerial viewpoint, and on the basis of actual business experience, came into its own. Harvard's famous 'case method', in which students were required to analyse the problems faced and decisions taken in real-life situations, became the pattern of instruction at many leading schools.

The status of undergraduate business education, which accounts for 90 per cent of the nearly 60,000 degrees in business that are awarded each year, has remained low. A course in business is sometimes regarded as a 'soft option' for less talented undergraduates. While standards vary widely in undergraduate schools, a bachelor's degree in business is not usually viewed as a good preparation for a master's degree; the leading graduate schools often prefer students who studied 'liberal arts' at the undergraduate level.

The whole field of business education has been subjected to persistent criticism and scrutiny. Two full-scale studies[6] financed by the Ford and Carnegie Foundations and published in 1959 have led to an extensive reappraisal of teaching methods and curriculum content. But it is widely accepted that the work of the leading graduate schools, about a score in number, has improved, to a significant though unmeasurable extent, the quality of management in American industry. These are at the universities which either confine their business education to the graduate level (like Harvard, Stanford, Chicago, Columbia and Cornell), or keep their graduate schools distinct from undergraduate business education (like Carnegie Institute of Technology, Massachusetts Institute of Technology, New York University and University of California).

At first it may have been hoped that out of the study of particular business cases certain general rules could be drawn up which would constitute a 'science' of business administration. Instead, the case method came to be valued principally as training in the 'art' of decision-making. Yet as the study of business progressed, art was increasingly supplemented by knowledge. Several business schools, notably at Chicago, Carnegie Institute of Technology, and M.I.T., moved in a different direction from Harvard and stressed the application of mathematical techniques to management problems.

These techniques, sometimes involving the use of electronic computers to make complicated calculations very quickly, have been successfully applied to such operations as the control of stocks and the scheduling of production. Decisions which had been left to the 'judgement' of production control managers or warehouse managers can be broken down into their constituent elements, and the information which had guided the managers can be analysed more accurately, and acted on more rapidly, by the computer. In some processes the computer can receive an order from a customer and relay the appropriate instructions to the factory floor.

Under the generic name of 'operations research', these techniques involve the rigorous, logical analysis of all the factors that go into a decision, eliminating the 'rule-of-thumb' judgements on which the manager had previously relied. Operations research in business involves the application of scientific attitudes and scientific techniques to business problems. For example, a company which makes a variety of products at several different locations needs to know how to distribute the products among the plants and among warehouses so that the delivered cost of each item to the customer can be reduced to the minimum. Operations research can be used to work out the manufacturing and warehousing arrangements that will best meet this objective. Again, a paper manufacturer which wants to reduce its waste costs needs to analyse the individual customer orders so that its production schedules are arranged in the most efficient manner; here, as in many applications of operations research, a computer can work out the complicated calculations with speed and efficiency.

The study of operations research has advanced rapidly since the war, and there are two professional societies in the field, the Operations Research Society and the Institute of Management Sciences, both of which publish their own journals. A number of quantitative tools have been developed to aid the businessman in his decision-making. The Critical Path Method, for example, is a technique for analysing, planning and scheduling a large project such as the construction of a building or the installation of a computer system. It involves the isolation of those steps in the process which are 'critical' in terms of their effect on the total amount of time which the project takes to complete, and the scheduling of all the critical steps along a 'path' which provides for the completion of the project in the shortest possible time and at the minimum cost. A related technique is PERT (Programme Evaluation Review Technique) which was first developed in the U.S. Navy's Polaris submarine programme. This, too, enables a manager to plan a complex operation in a logical way, to foresee the impact of variations from the plan and to take corrective action promptly. Its use is gradually spreading from military to business applications.

The choice between alternative capital investment opportunities – one of the most crucial decisions the manager has to make – is another field where the use of mathematical techniques has been growing. Instead of the simple 'pay-off' period to judge whether a piece of machinery should be replaced, more sophisticated 'discounted cash flow' techniques have been developed, in which the savings expected over the life of the new piece of equipment, taking account of taxation, tax reliefs and depreciation, are balanced against its capital cost. But a decision to introduce a new product or to invade a new market is complicated by a large number of variables – what the firm's share of the market is likely to be, how fast the market will grow, how the price level will change, and so on. Mathematical techniques can be used to assess the degree of uncertainty attached to each variable and to isolate the known from the unknown so that, though judgement is still required, it will be based on as much information as can be obtained. Similar techniques can guide a company in choosing between alternative research projects.

The ultimate impact of these techniques on management is hard to assess. According to one authority,[7] American industry is 'in the early stages of a technological revolution of the decision-making process', and computers will eventually graduate from operations research to 'heuristic programming', in which they will incorporate the 'art of plausible reasoning' and acquire the capacity to solve relatively 'ill-structured' problems. Some even suggest that the top managers of the future will be drawn from experts in operations research and computer specialists, instead of the lawyers, accountants and engineers who fill many of the top positions today. Another possibility is that the new techniques will lead to the 'recentralization' of large enterprises, as the top managers, freed of much routine decision-making and making use of the latest data-processing techniques, acquire the ability to act on a wider range of problems and to exercise closer supervision over their subordinate divisions.

It seems possible that advances along these lines may reduce the importance of 'middle management' in the company organization, just as Taylor's contributions to scientific management virtually eliminated the initiative and judgement required of the hourly worker.[8] But as far as top management is concerned, the new techniques will never be a complete substitute for the essential qualities of perception and judgement. The computer will become increasingly useful as an aid to management, but it will not take over the job of management.

In business education, the debate continues between advocates of the case method and the 'mathematical' school, but it is clear that the two approaches are complementary. The Harvard Business School has been revising its curriculum to include more of the new techniques, modifying but not eliminating its dependence on the case method. A former dean of the Harvard Business School has suggested that management, which is 90 per cent art and 10 per cent science today, might become 80 per cent art and 20 per cent science after another generation.

In addition to their training in the art and science of decision-making, a major contribution of the business schools has been their intensive research into the conditions which determine the performance of business enterprises and the effectiveness of their management. These studies are made possible by the willingness of most companies to submit their problems, past and present, to the scrutiny of business school teachers and students. The liaison between business and business schools is not yet as close as, say between medicine and the medical schools, but both sides are endeavouring to improve the channels of communication. Some teachers serve as industrial consultants or on the boards of companies. This applies as much to the engineering and scientific departments of the university as to the business schools, and is in marked contrast to the situation in Britain, where the gulf between the academic and business worlds has yet to be bridged. At the business schools company executives often participate with the students in discussions of their own 'cases'; many businessmen have been able to improve their organization as a result of the investigations carried out on their premises by business school students. Still greater mobility between university and business is regarded as desirable. Many schools offer short courses for middle and senior management which provide businessmen with an opportunity to keep up to date and to take a broader view of their particular company problems. They enable a man

to rub his mind against the minds of executives from other industries, companies, functions and places. His imagination is stirred by discovering that other organizations, facing problems similar to those confronted by his own firm, have used different solutions successfully. Formally and informally, in daytime classes and night-time bull sessions, his thinking is challenged, prodded, stimulated, exercised and broadened.[9]

These courses supplement the educational work of professional organizations like the American Management Association. This body, founded in 1923, has made spectacular progress in the past twenty years. Besides its educational programmes, the pooling of knowledge in such fields as labour relations, marketing and finance which takes place at A.M.A. gatherings helps to disseminate throughout industry an awareness of new ideas and new methods for handling management problems.

Important contributions to 'managerial knowledge' have also been made by the management consultants. There is plenty of quackery in this field, and the search for acceptable professional standards has proved almost as difficult as in management itself. Consultants are expensive and the results of their inquiries are often disappointing. Companies often benefit from an objective look at their business by outsiders – 'you've taught us how to think' is a common reaction – but consultants are sometimes used as weapons in internal company politics.

There is no doubt, nevertheless, that firms like McKinsey; Booz, Allen & Hamilton; and Cresap, McCormick & Paget have contributed towards the wider acceptance of a scientific approach to business problems. To some extent they provide a link between business and the business schools. The consulting firms often recruit business school graduates who have had no practical business experience, in the belief that the analytical, problem-solving qualities required in the successful consultant are not necessarily the qualities required in the successful executive.

Though consultants are often called in to assist ailing companies, the bulk of their business is said to be with successful and efficient concerns, which know enough about their business to know where their shortcomings are and to recognize the scope for improvement. For example, the General Foods–McKinsey study of food distribution* is an example of a scientific study which can sometimes be conducted more effectively by an outside consultant than by participants in the industry. Booz, Allen & Hamilton played a leading part, in conjunction with Lockheed and the U.S. Navy, in developing the PERT technique, and subsequently in applying the technique to industrial problems. A firm like Arthur D. Little, with special expertise in research and development, accumulates considerable experience of companies' problems and attempted solutions, from which rules of conduct can sometimes be derived.

Is Management A Profession?

Despite the growth of business education and managerial knowledge, America is a long way from the day when professional training is a necessary prerequisite for admission to a business career, let alone for success in it. There are many unresolved questions – over the content of the curriculum, over the degree of

*See page 33.

specialization, over the kind of undergraduate training which should precede entry to a graduate business school, and so on. These uncertainties stem in part from the failure to define the qualities needed in the successful manager and the conditions necessary for a successful enterprise. But the lack of definitive answers has not lessened the value of an analytical study of all the factors that affect business performance. While there is no formally agreed programme of training and no systematic body of managerial knowledge, there is in progress a gradual professionalization of management which is altering the character of American business. Business-school graduates may not always be the most successful businessmen (though there is some evidence that they are more mobile, more self-confident, and more willing to take risks[10]), and they are still a minority among top executives, but the rational approach to management which they represent seems to be gaining acceptance throughout industry.

In Britain and other European countries there is intense interest in American management techniques. The demand for management consultants, especially American ones, is growing rapidly. Business schools are to be established in London and Manchester. There is general agreement that an improvement in the quality of management will make a major contribution to Britain's economic progress. Many British companies are organized very loosely, with no clear lines of authority and no clear allocation of responsibilities. Instead of assigning an individual to a specific function and defining that function as precisely as possible, as is the American approach, British managers are often given vague 'troubleshooting' assignments covering a wide area. In a well-managed American company each key executive knows precisely what his function is and what his objectives are; if he fails to achieve them, he may lose his job. Rewards for success are higher than in Britain, but failure is punished more ruthlessly, even when the most senior executives are involved.

The application of reason to management decisions will not, of course, ensure that the decision will always be right. Disastrous mistakes can be made through faulty calculations of likely demand. Ford lost an estimated $350 million on the Edsel car and General Dynamics over $400 million on the Convair airliner. But the clinical analysis of mistakes like these helps to identify the areas where forecasting was weak and to suggest possible improvements. The success of Ford's Mustang car, introduced in 1964, may have owed something to the lessons learned after the Edsel fiasco.[11]

However foolproof a business organization may be on paper, it can often be frustrated by poor communications between line and staff, internal jockeying for position, and similar human problems. But here, too, the study of management experience sheds light on these human failings and reveals ways of countering them. The question of what makes a manager work hard, how to stimulate him to do better, and how to assess his performance in the job is being constantly studied and clarified.

All businesses are concerned, to a greater or lesser extent, with planning for the future. The 'budgeting' process, once confined to the control of costs, is now concerned with all the variables which will determine the success or failure of the enterprise in the future. The ability to influence some of these variables (like the level of consumer demand for a particular product) is always limited, because the firm operates in an environment which it can never completely control. The objective of the professional manager is to take the guesswork out of some of these planning decisions and to increase the area of decision-making which is subject to rational analysis.

All businesses are concerned, too, with improving the efficiency of their own organization. It is possible to build into the organization institutional pressures for greater efficiency which may be a partial substitute for, or at least reinforce, external competitive pressures. The sole purpose of industrial engineering departments in many firms is to make a continuous search for ways of cutting costs.

Knowledge about how to run a successful business is gradually being enlarged. The solution of management problems requires a faculty for judgement which is partly inborn but which can be developed and improved by training. In most cases it requires a substantial amount of knowledge, involving both the subject-matter of the problem (marketing, labour relations, finance or whatever it might be) and the availability of problem-solving techniques. The wisdom of the decision depends more on judgement than on knowledge, but both are usually essential in the successful manager, just as they are in the successful doctor or lawyer. The advance of knowledge does not necessarily make the manager's task easier – a reasoned decision may be harder work than an intuitive decision – and it rarely provides a guaranteed solution to a specific problem. But just as the study of medicine increases man's knowledge of the causes of diseases and the cure for them, so the scientific study of business extends man's knowledge of the reasons for the success and failure of business enterprises and of the courses of action which should be encouraged or avoided.

The idea that business is becoming professionalized is often attacked on the ground that it implies the gradual disappearance of the 'profit motive' as the primary concern of the businessman. Both critics and supporters of the 'free enterprise system' often associate the profit motive with the desire for personal enrichment, as if the businessman was necessarily, by virtue of the occupation he has chosen, entirely devoted to making money for himself. In practice, the typical corporation manager is primarily concerned with the success and hence the profitability of the corporation for which he works. To this goal he may bring the same dedication, the same qualities of perception and judgement backed by professional training, that the doctor brings to the practice of medicine.

It is true that, whether or not he owns stock in the company, the businessman is likely to benefit personally from its success, since his own earnings are usually tied in some way to the profits of the enterprise. That the businessman is influenced by the hope of financial gain is an assumption inherent in the 'profit centre' approach to decentralization, whereby the division manager is responsible for the division's profitability and benefits personally if the division prospers. Most companies share General Motors' view that 'the most effective results and the maximum progress and stability of the business are achieved by placing its executives in the same relative position, so far as possible, that they would occupy if they were conducting a business on their own account'. But most doctors, most lawyers, are also in business for their own account, and they, too, are influenced by the hope of financial gain. The doctor and the business executive may both combine altruism and greed in about the same proportion.

8 · The International Corporation

The Growth of Foreign Investments

'WE think of ourselves, not as an American company with overseas interests, but as an international company whose headquarters happen to be in the United States.' This claim, made by the head of a large chemical company and shared by a growing number of firms, reflects a new attitude towards overseas business which has emerged during the past fifteen years. Many companies which had thought of foreign markets merely as convenient outlets for their surplus production now regard their overseas business as an integral part of their total operations. They have discovered that handsome profits can be made by treating a foreign market with the same degree of care and attention that they apply to the various segments of the American market. They are beginning to look at all aspects of their business – purchasing, manufacturing, selling, research, recruitment, finance – from a global point of view.

Few American companies are yet as fully 'international' as European firms like Royal Dutch Shell, Unilever, Nestles and Philips, but the trend is accelerating. Already a large number of companies, including such well-known names as Burroughs, Colgate–Palmolive, Heinz, Hoover, International Telephone and Telegraph, National Cash Register, Pfizer, Royal McBee, Socony Mobil, Standard Oil of New Jersey, and Woolworth, derive over half their profits from abroad. Some 500 companies do at least $10 million of overseas business each year, and more than 3,000 firms are believed to own foreign subsidiaries. Investing abroad has become fashionable. Phrases like 'the multinational corporation' and 'international people's capitalism' have become the stock-in-trade of speakers at management conferences and writers in management journals.

The 'internationalization' of business has presented American management with unfamiliar and complex problems. Running a world enterprise is harder work than running a domestic company. It is often difficult to graft a growing overseas business on to an existing organizational framework. The problem of communication between foreign managers and the central office, the degree of decentralization that is feasible or desirable, the coordination of investment and sales decisions, all this requires an administrative skill which is difficult for a domestically oriented company to acquire. There are political problems involved in dealing with foreign governments. Quite apart from tax laws and currency regulations which may be changed to suit the government's convenience, public and private attitudes to American investors may be unfriendly. Within the U.S. the growth of foreign investment has incurred the displeasure both of the Federal Government (because of its impact on the balance of payments deficit) and of the labour unions, which have been troubled by the 'export' of jobs.

Despite these difficulties, the surge of interest in overseas business is not likely to be temporary. As artificial barriers to trade and investment are brought down, the economies of the non-Communist nations will become more interdependent. The business of selling cars or computers or shoes is already becoming international in scope; a company that wishes to participate fully in the business cannot restrict its operations to a single country, even a country as large as the United States.

Although Tiffany, the jewellers, opened a Paris store in 1850, it was only at the close of the nineteenth century that American companies began to invest overseas on a significant scale. In 1900 European investment in the U.S. was far larger than American investment in Europe, but firms like Singer, National Cash Register, Standard Oil, Eastman Kodak, and General Electric were beginning to develop their international activities. In Latin America and Canada, too, American capital was moving into railways, plantations, mining, and other basic industries. After the First World War American investment in Europe rose sharply, partly because high tariffs were keeping out exports, partly because of a growing shortage of capital in Europe.

General Motors, for example, had developed a substantial export business in Europe, but the trade was vulnerable to economic nationalism and rising tariffs. Local assembly of American-built components was only a partial answer, and the company soon decided that the way to participate on a permanent basis in the fast-growing European market was to invest in full-scale local production. After abortive negotiations with Citroen in France and Austin in Britain, the company purchased Opel in Germany and Vauxhall in Britain.[1] Like other American concerns, General Motors was primarily concerned with profiting from the European demand for cars, but in later years its European plants were also used to supply the U.S. market with small cars which could not be economically manufactured in domestic factories.

By 1929 over 1,300 European companies were owned or controlled by American firms, representing the first stage in the American 'invasion' of European industry. Even at this early stage there was an ambivalent attitude on the part of many Europeans to American investment. The benefits to be derived from American techniques of mass production, standardization, and scientific management were acknowledged, but there were fears of domination by American industrial giants. In the U.S., too, the labour unions were alarmed. The American Federation of Labour pressed unsuccessfully for the inclusion in a 1930 tariff bill of a clause that would have prohibited the importation into the U.S. of goods manufactured in American-owned plants overseas.

The Depression and the Second World War held the invasion in check. Between 1929 and 1946 the value of direct investments by American companies in foreign countries declined slightly from $7,500 million to $7,200 million. In the years immediately following the war steps were taken to revive and enlarge existing investments, both in manufacturing and in extractive industries. By 1950 the value of foreign investments had climbed to $11,800 million, more than half of which was concentrated in Latin America and Canada. U.S. investment in Latin America was largely concerned with the exploitation of raw materials – oil, copper, iron ore, bauxite, bananas and other agricultural products – which were either unavailable or in short supply in the United States. Investments in public utilities, such as electricity and telecommunications, were also considerable. In Canada, too, investments in mining and in oil were on a large scale, but because of the nearness of the market and the similarity in living standards manufacturing investments were more important than in Latin America.

During the 1950s Europe began to assume much greater importance as a target for American investment. The rapid rise in living standards made Europe ripe for the mass-produced consumer goods and sophisticated capital equipment in which American manufacturers excelled. While some of these goods could be

TABLE 6

Growth of foreign investments 1929–64

($000m., book values)

	1929	1946	1950	1964
Total	7·5	7·2	11·8	44·3
Areas				
Canada	2·0	2·5	3·6	13·8
Latin America	3·5	3·1	4·6	8·9
Europe	1·4	1·0	1·7	12·1*
Middle East and Africa	·1	·2	1·0	2·9
Other areas	·5	·4	·9	6·6
Industries				
Manufacturing	1·8	2·4	3·8	16·9
Petroleum	1·1	1·4	3·4	14·4
Mining and Smelting	1·2	·8	1·1	3·6
Public Utilities	1·6	1·3	1·4	2·0
Other industries	1·8	1·3	2·1	7·4

*Although new U.S. investment in the Common Market has been growing faster than in Britain during the last few years, the value of American investments in Britain amounts to $4,600 million, compared to $2,100 million in Germany and $1,400 million in France.

supplied from plants inside the U.S., it soon became necessary for many firms to establish their own base of production in Europe. This was partly because high tariffs discriminated against imports. The formation of the Common Market, leading to an eventual common external tariff, gave an impetus to American investment; once they were established inside the European Economic Community, U.S. firms could look forward to the emergence of a tariff-free Continental market even bigger than the United States itself.

As long as the American product had a significant edge in price or quality over the locally made product, direct exports from the U.S. could continue. But in several fields the foreign producer was catching up with his American rival. He was offering a product that was as good as the American's, and he had the advantage of local affiliations and nearness to the customer. The American supplier often had to choose between withdrawing from the market and investing in local production. Sometimes, too, the foreign market required a different product from the U.S. For example, the rise in Europe's demand for cars during the 1950s did not create new opportunities for American exports. U.S.-built cars were too expensive and too large to be sold effectively in Europe where there was a premium on economy in petrol consumption; American companies could only share in the European car boom by expanding their European factories.

In some cases competition from imports forced American producers to switch part of their production for the U.S. market to overseas factories. Manufacturers of shoes, apparel, and watches, for example, having lost part of their home market to Swiss, Italian and other foreign-made goods, began to produce in the United States only those items where they had an advantage over the foreigner, and to use their foreign plants for the rest. Because of the disparity in labour costs, conventional typewriters could be produced more cheaply in Europe than in the United States; instead of simply abandoning the U.S. typewriter market to foreign companies, American firms could establish or acquire their own plants in Europe. Burroughs Corporation could make adding machines in Scotland at a cost that was 40 per cent less than in Detroit. Hence it decided to close its Detroit plant and supply the U.S. adding-machine market from Scotland. At the same time Burroughs continued to manufacture computers in the U.S. and export them to Europe. Products with a high labour content could often be produced economically overseas, where wages were lower than in the U.S. More advanced products with a high 'technological' content could still be produced in the U.S. and exported. Although America's share of total world exports of manufactures declined from 25 per cent to 20 per cent between 1954 and 1964 (while Britain's share dropped from 20 per cent to 15 per cent), her competitive strength, based primarily on advanced products, ensured a substantial trade surplus.

Between 1950 and 1964 the value of direct investment in foreign countries rose from $11,800 million to $44,300 million. A group of 100 major companies surveyed by McKinsey, the management consultants, increased their foreign sales by 275 per cent between 1950 and 1962; in the same period their domestic sales rose by only 40 per cent. As a proportion of their foreign sales, direct exports from the U.S. fell from 38 per cent to 29 per cent during this period; their volume of exports in 1962 was 2·7 times what it had been in 1950, but the output of their foreign plants was 4·2 times higher. Although the survey showed wide variations in the profitability of overseas operations, most of the firms made more profit on their foreign production than on their domestic sales or on their exports.

The motives for establishing a manufacturing plant overseas are numerous. Sometimes a company may wish to diversify so as to lessen its dependence on unstable or cyclical markets at home; the machine-tool makers, for example, whose order book is subject to extreme fluctuations, could reasonably expect that a boom or recession in the U.S. market would not coincide with exactly similar conditions in the European market, where several of them are now established. Sometimes a company has surplus cash and cannot find profitable outlets for it in the U.S. There is, too, a strong imitative element in U.S. foreign investment. It has become fashionable to be a 'multinational' corporation; lack of overseas interests, like the lack of research facilities, is sometimes regarded as a sign of backwardness. Once one firm in an industry establishes itself in the Common Market, its competitors feel obliged to do likewise. Sometimes a firm may be barred by the antitrust laws from expanding its own line of business in the U.S.; hence it looks overseas for growth. The international habit is spreading to basic industries like steel (which had hitherto looked to overseas countries mainly as a source of raw materials) and to non-manufacturing industries like retailing; in the last few years the largest mail order company (Sears Roebuck), a leading supermarket group (Safeway), and a leading discounter (Gem International) have taken steps to establish themselves in Europe. The banks, too, have opened a large number of overseas branches.

But perhaps the biggest stimulus to overseas investment has been the rapid economic growth in many foreign countries compared to the more pedestrian rate of advance in the United States. In the U.S. the demand for many consumer products like cars and washing machines has reached a stage of maturity, growing at a slow rate linked to the increase of population and the need for replacement. Just as European demand for energy is growing by 4 per cent a year compared to 3 per cent a year in the U.S., so many manufacturing firms see overseas markets as a source of dynamic growth which is no longer easily obtainable in the U.S. There are still less than half as many cars and refrigerators per person in Europe as in the U.S.

Despite the lack of pattern the effect of the recent surge in overseas investment has been to 'internationalize' certain product markets and the companies which serve them. Massey-Ferguson, the Canadian farm equipment producer, is one of the companies which has gone furthest in the direction of a global strategy, whereby product planning, manufacturing and marketing are rationalized and integrated in a network of factories throughout the world. A similar approach to tractor production for world markets has recently been adopted by Ford.

The Developing Countries

As American companies expand their worldwide operations, competition for locally-owned firms becomes intense. Fears grow that the American giants will dominate the local economy and that the country's economic and industrial independence will disappear. The problem is especially serious in the developing countries where American concerns, often involved in basic industries, may exert a preponderant influence on the domestic economy. The companies often have legacies from the 'exploitative' past, when they could virtually control, in colonial fashion, the local governments. Their concern was with the resources that could be extracted from the 'host' country, or with the profits that could be made in it, and they had no allegiance to the country itself. As Samuel Zemurray, chairman of United Fruit, the great banana-producing company which dominated the economies of several Central American countries, put it in the 1930s:

I feel guilty about some of the things we did; all we cared about was dividends. Well, you can't do business that way today. We have learned that what's best for the countries we operate in is best for the company. Maybe we can't make the people love us, but we will make ourselves so useful to them that they will want us to stay.

A drastic change in attitude was necessary if companies like United Fruit were to live down their colonial past and find a way of cooperating with the nationalist movements that gradually assumed control in the developing countries. The prolonged struggle between the oil companies and the Mexican Government, which eventually resulted in their expropriation in 1938, illustrated the futility of the policy of adamant resistance to nationalist demands. It was difficult for 'old timers' in the business to accept some of the new demands that were made, and the clash was sometimes violent, as in Cuba. But despite the Cuban episode, in which American oil companies and other enterprises were nationalized, there was a growing realization in the postwar period that a new attitude was essential.

United Fruit, for example, which had become the symbol of colonial exploitation (though its actual performance hardly justified its reputation), tried to develop a policy of 'partnership' with local governments. It modified its labour relations policies and tried to stimulate local proprietorship in banana production.

In Chile the American copper companies were faced with steadily rising taxes and the constant threat of nationalization. Fluctuations in the price of copper had severe effects on the Chilean economy, but attempts by the Government to control the price caused Chile's share of world copper exports to drop. The companies were accused of using their Chilean profits to finance the construction of refining facilities in the U.S., and they were urged to re-invest more in Chile itself. Relations between the government and the companies were never stable, and there were signs in the early 1960s that the companies would switch some of their exploration efforts from Chile to the U.S. and Canada. In 1964, however, a presidential election in Chile resulted in the defeat of the proponent of outright nationalization. The new president, Señor Frei, negotiated a new arrangement with the companies whereby, in return for lower taxes, the Chilean Government acquired a large financial interest in the American-owned mines. This step towards the 'Chileanization' of the mines provided a means whereby the companies and the government could live together, though in view of the uncertain political situation it was not clear how permanent the arrangement would be.

Chile's bargaining position was weakened by the fact that it was responsible for less than 20 per cent of the world's copper production; if production in Chile became too risky or unprofitable, copper production in other countries could be stepped up. In crude oil this problem was tackled by cooperation among the producing countries. The Organization of Petroleum Exporting Countries was established in order to bargain with the oil companies for better terms. Here again outright nationalization was unlikely to be successful, since the companies controlled the marketing and distribution of crude oil. But a united front by the producing governments helped to strengthen their negotiating position. They were assisted, too, by the entry into the world oil business of new companies – American, Italian, French and Japanese – which were often willing to form partnerships with state-owned firms and move away from the traditional fifty–fifty profit-sharing arrangements that had been the rule.

The oil companies operate on a worldwide scale, and it is usually necessary for them to have full control of their production facilities: a local or governmental shareholding in one particular area, such as Venezuela, may make it difficult for the company to coordinate its worldwide production in the most efficient manner. Hence the companies generally resist such local shareholdings in production, though it has sometimes been conceded in refining operations where the local government insists on it. Yet the charge of exploitation is frequently made, and the companies have had to find ways of meeting it. In one case Creole Petroleum, the subsidiary of Standard Oil of New Jersey in Venezuela, has used its oil profits to re-invest in other industrial enterprises, thus demonstrating its desire to promote the Venezuelan economy as a whole.

Some companies involved in basic industries, such as public utilities, have bowed to nationalist pressure and voluntarily sold their enterprises to the local government. In Latin America such companies as American and Foreign Power (once the largest utility in the continent) and International Telephone and Telegraph, have sold certain installations to governments and have re-invested the proceeds in industrial enterprises – from which they could often get a higher return than in the public utility field, where they were constantly subject to government pressure and various forms of price control.

A flexible approach is clearly needed if American companies are to operate profitably and harmoniously in a developing country. In recent years much of the new investment in these areas has been in manufacturing; the new investors have no 'exploitative' past to live down and they are interested not in extracting something from the country but in participating in that country's economic growth. They are more pragmatic in their attitude to joint ventures with local businessmen or with the local government; a new flour mill to be built by Pillsbury in Ghana is to be owned 60 per cent by the Ghanaian Government, 40 per cent by the American company. Although some companies insist on complete control of all their overseas interests, there are signs of a trend towards more joint ventures, especially in the developing countries.

As an official of Celanese Corporation remarked:

I have a strong opinion that every company establishing a manufacturing facility in Mexico, or anywhere else for that matter, should organize it as a venture jointly owned with local capital. In the first place, the capital is available. In the second place, it becomes possible to stimulate national pride when selling the product. Local partners will help one avoid mistakes and handle local problems better than we. An affiliated company is not likely to become a political target, whereas a foreign subsidiary may become fair game for anyone.[2]

Some manufacturing firms, like W. R. Grace in Peru, have successfully integrated themselves into the local economy, strengthening their ties with local industry by buying goods and services from local suppliers, staffing their plants and offices with local personnel, and using local contractors wherever possible. In this way the nationality of the enterprise may be forgotten, and the danger of anti-American attitudes is lessened. If the product is in some way basic to the economy or a subject of political debate (such as foodstuffs, drugs, or steel), the need for circumspection and the advisability of joint ventures is much greater.

The foreign investor must be able to demonstrate, in concrete terms, that his activities benefit the host country as much as his own shareholders. The heritage of past exploitation has to be recognized as part of the environment. The political instability of some developing countries carries risks (though the risks of doing business in Latin America may be no greater than doing business for the Defence Department, where the sudden cancellation of orders can have disastrous consequences on investments), and the right to nationalize has to be acknowledged. A rigid insistence on 100 per cent ownership may oblige a company to abandon opportunities in countries where joint ventures are compulsory, or may lead to a conflict of interests that could end in expropriation.

Global Planning

Similar political problems may be encountered in the industrialized countries. In Canada, for example, where American-owned companies hold a dominant position in many sectors of industry, there have been proposals that locally-owned companies should be protected, by a 'take-over' tax or in some other way, from being acquired or controlled by companies south of the border. American firms have been encouraged to sell minority share-holdings to Canadian investors. There have been complaints that American companies employ too few Canadians, conduct too little research in Canada, and do not contribute enough to Canadian exports. These anti-American attitudes have persisted, but the country's need for outside capital to develop her resources is so great that very little defensive action has been taken.

The influx of American companies into Europe during the past decade has revived fears of economic domination from across the Atlantic. In France, especially, General de Gaulle's pursuit of independence from the United States in the political and military spheres has been supplemented by a more critical attitude towards direct American investment. There are fears that if the invasion of American capital is not checked the United States will assume responsibility for the economies of Europe as it already has strategic responsibility for peace and war. It has been estimated that American capital represents only about 1 per cent of the total capital invested in Europe, whereas European investment in the United States during the nineteenth century accounted for as much as 15 per cent of the total capital invested in the country. But this does nothing to allay the uneasiness which many foreigners feel when American companies acquire a dominant position in a major industry.

In a recent speech the French Minister of Industry praised the contributions which American companies have made to French technological advance, but insisted that there were dangers in permitting uncontrolled foreign investment. He deplored the transfer to the United States of centres of decision and the assignment to parent companies of research and the 'noblest' functions of management, leaving to its subsidiary the 'secondary chores'. It is felt that decisions taken by the parent company, which may have manufacturing operations in several different countries, may not always be in the best interests of one particular country. It may decide to expand faster in one country than another, or to export more from one plant than another. The subsidiary company is subject to the authority of the local government, and both subsidiary and parent are usually willing to cooperate with the government's policies on, for example, the dispersion of industry away from the metropolitan regions. But the managers of a global enterprise are primarily concerned with the health of the enterprise as a whole; they have no special allegiance to any one country or plant.

In Britain, for example, there is an urgent need to improve the balance of payments. Many American-owned companies, especially the vehicle manufacturers, have made impressive contributions to the export drive; some of them, indeed, are more successful exporters than their locally-owned rivals, partly because they are more efficient, partly because they can make use of the parent company's worldwide marketing organization. But there are times when the parent finds it more profitable to supply a particular export market or group of markets from, say, the German plant instead of the British plant; decisions of this kind may have adverse effects on the British balance of payments, at least in the short term. Clearly the European subsidiaries of Ford and General Motors do not have the same freedom in attacking the United States market as, for example, British Motor Corporation or Volkswagen.

Similarly, Britain, like other European countries, is eager to develop her science-based industries, like electronics and computers, which are likely to contribute both to the export drive and to the progressiveness of the economy as a whole. American companies are often more advanced in these fields than their European rivals. In computers European-owned companies have found it difficult to hold their own against competition from International Business Machines, which has over 70 per cent of the U.S. market and an even larger share of the world market. The going has, of course, been no easier for I.B.M.'s rivals in the domestic market; such powerful companies as General Electric, Radio Corporation of America, and Sperry Rand have had to sustain several years of heavy losses in their attempt to establish a position in the computer field. But the demand for computers in the United States, assisted by the Government's space and defence programmes, is very much larger than in Europe and should provide room for several competing companies, though not as many as are now in the business; there are eight major contenders, and this number may be halved through mergers or acquisitions during the next decade.

In Europe the market is smaller, government requirements are less significant, and the management of computer manufacturers appears to have been weaker. Bull of France and Olivetti of Italy found it impossible to maintain their independence; their computer divisions have been reinforced by capital and know-how from an American company, General Electric. Britain is now the only non-Communist country apart from the United States which has a native computer industry. Whether the principal manufacturers, English Electric–Leo–Marconi, International Computers and Tabulators, Ferranti and Elliot-Automation, can survive the intense competition that lies ahead is uncertain. In the belief that an advanced industrial country should not depend on the Americans for technological progress in the computer field, the British Government intends to foster the development of the industry; it is providing funds for research and development and is encouraging government departments and other users to 'buy British'. These measures of protection, it is hoped, will provide a breathing space in which the British computer industry can establish itself more securely. Many Americans, however, believe that the prospects for any European computer maker will be dim unless it is linked to, though not necessarily controlled by, an American company.

There is no doubt that Europeans have received far more from the American invaders than they have lost in the way of economic independence. Suspicion about the motives and policies of American companies is often unjustified. But it exists; it is part of the environment to which the international company has to adapt. The problem is less acute for companies which have been so long established overseas that their American origin is almost forgotten. International Telephone and Telegraph, for example, probably has the largest manufacturing operation in Europe of any American company except for Ford and General Motors; it is believed to account for about a third of the European telephone-equipment market. But its subsidiaries, such as Standard Telephones and Cables in Britain, are hardly recognized as American. But for a newcomer, like Chrysler in the motor industry, the problem of nationalism is more serious. The only route open to Chrysler was to buy a partial shareholding in existing companies – Rootes in Britain and Simca in France. In Simca Chrysler now has a controlling interest, but control of Rootes is shared with the Rootes family.

Naturally a partnership between an American and a local company is much less objectionable on nationalistic grounds; for this reason some firms deliberately steer clear of wholly-owned subsidiaries. The case for joint ventures in industrialized as well as the developing countries is strong. Local investors can share in the profits and participate in the decisions. The stigma of foreign ownership is avoided. The American contributes his knowhow and experience, while his partner provides knowledge of local conditions. Capital and management can be obtained locally; good relations with the public and the government can be established.

In Japan foreign companies are prohibited from owning more than 50 per cent of a manufacturing or marketing operation. Perhaps because partnerships are mandatory, they have worked less well here than in some other countries. American companies which had built up a large export trade with Japan or which had licensed products and processes to Japanese companies, have wanted to participate more directly in Japan's spectacular economic growth, but the necessity to work with Japanese partners has often proved difficult. It seems that the Japanese business system, the relationships between firms and between management and labour, the traditional marketing arrangements, are so different from the U.S. that the American newcomer cannot make the necessary adjustments. In recent years there have been signs of a rather more liberal attitude on the part of the Japanese authorities towards joint ventures with American companies. But foreign investments are still generally limited to a narrow product range and to industries which are structurally solid, containing powerful companies well able to stand up to the

Americans. While they are eager to learn from the Americans, the Japanese intend to keep firm control over their own technology. It does not appear that the progress of the Japanese economy has suffered as a result of this restrictive policy.

A majority of American companies, including such large overseas investors as General Motors, Ford, and International Business Machines, strongly favour 100 per cent ownership of foreign subsidiaries. 'Divided ownership results in a tangled skein of corporate relations', according to a Ford official; 'if you're going to be truly global, you need the freedom of action that comes largely from establishing 100 per cent ownership'. Ford's decision to buy out the local shareholders in its British company (just as General Motors had bought out the minority holding in its Australian subsidiary) reflected its desire to exercise tighter control over all its overseas operations. Its principal overseas companies had been run largely as autonomous enterprises, supported but not closely supervised by the parent company in the U.S. The new 'global' orientation which Ford, like other companies, was beginning to adopt involved the coordination of all overseas activities from the company's headquarters; the autonomy of the local managers, as far as the key policy decisions were concerned, was curtailed.

These '100 per cent only' companies are aware of the problem of nationalism, but their answer to it is not to form partnerships with local investors, but to encourage the international ownership of shares in the parent corporation. This is the concept of 'international people's capitalism' of which General Motors, in particular, is a strong advocate. 'The day must come', says Arthur K. Watson of I.B.M., 'when people no longer point to corporations and say that it is American or British or German or Japanese. If a company does business throughout the world, it should be owned throughout the world'. The shares of some U.S. companies are traded in London and other foreign stock exchanges, and a gradual diffusion of share-ownership is taking place. This process, if it continues, will ensure that the dividends are shared among the citizens of countries where the companies do business. But it does not alter the fact that the key policy decisions will continue to be taken by the parent company at its headquarters in the U.S.

This will continue, because a worldwide enterprise has to be coordinated from one central point. The top management will be subject to pressure from local governments and local shareholders, but it will not be controlled by them. As a leading consultant to international companies has said:

> The really decisive point in the transition to world enterprise is top-management recognition that, to function effectively, the ultimate control of strategic planning and policy decisions must shift from decentralized subsidiaries or division locations to corporate headquarters, where a worldwide perspective can be brought to bear on the interests of the total enterprise.[3]

Some companies which have long been established in overseas manufacturing, such as Hoover, had allowed the lines of communication between head office and overseas subsidiaries to become loose. In Hoover's case the need to adopt a global viewpoint was not fully recognized, and relations between the corporate headquarters in the Midwest, the Hoover Worldwide Corporation in New York, and the highly profitable and independent-minded British subsidiary were unsatisfactory. More recently some firms, instead of handling their overseas business through a separate international division, adopted a 'product structure', whereby a division is given responsibility for manufacturing and selling a particular product, or group of products, on a worldwide basis, including the United States.[4] The Dow Chemical Company is one of several firms that are moving in this direction.

American industry is still in the early stages of 'going international'. The problem of organization, the question of partnerships as opposed to wholly-owned subsidiaries, is still unresolved. There is no doubt that in the next few decades the operations of a relatively small number of large international corporations, principally American, will assume an even greater importance in the world economy. Just as inside the U.S. the power and influence of firms like General Motors and General Electric exceeds that of some individual states, so on the world scene the international corporation will begin to exercise a kind of sovereignty of its own. Just how the essentially undemocratic nature of the corporation will be reconciled with the need for accountability to the countries in which it operates, remains to be seen. Some observers envisage an international tribunal which will arbitrate disputes between corporations and governments and will enforce a code of conduct for international enterprises.

The best American companies are bringing to international business the same flexible, pragmatic, rational approach which they apply to their domestic affairs. Changing political conditions can be dangerous, but the genuinely international corporation has a commitment to world business which enables it to look beyond short-term setbacks, whether economic or political. There is sometimes an element of crusade for 'the American free enterprise system' in management pronouncements about the value of foreign investment, but most American businessmen are much less doctrinaire in their attitude to socialism overseas than they are at home. They intend to seize business opportunities wherever they can be found; if the project involves a partnership with foreign governments, this is accepted as necessary and even desirable in some circumstances. They are naturally eager to preserve their autonomy, as they are in the U.S., and this can lead to clashes of will with the local government. But they are unlikely to engage in the kind of all-out resistance to local demands which the oil companies in Mexico attempted before the war. A commitment to international business involves a realistic assessment of the limits on the international company's freedom of action.

9 · Invention and Innovation

The Need for Research and Development

SUCCESS in a competitive business requires a continuous search for new products and processes. For most companies in most industries some attention to scientific research is essential for business survival. During the decade of the 1950s, expenditure on industrial research rose sharply; the percentage of sales spent on research by manufacturers went from 0·8 to 2·5.[1] As competition has intensified during the past few years, the need for research has been greater, but because the need is more widely recognized, it is increasingly difficult for any one company to maintain a technological lead over its rivals. Whereas before the war firms like General Electric and Du Pont were exceptional in their attention to scientific research, there are now a number of other large companies which are just as conscious of research and almost as successful at performing it. There is constant pressure not only to produce new inventions, but to shorten the time lag between test-tube and commercial utilization.

Business firms are the principal source of technological advance in the American economy. Although the role of the independent inventor is still important, there has been a marked shift of research effort from individuals to corporations. Only 40 per cent of all patents were issued to individuals in 1957, compared to 80 per cent in 1900. The growing complexity of industrial technology, the need to coordinate the work of specialists in several different fields, and the rising cost of research have increased the advantage which the large corporate laboratory enjoys over the private 'tinkerer'. The big corporation does not always provide a hospitable environment for the creative scientist; there is plenty of scope for small science-based firms which depend on the ingenuity of one or two outstanding individuals. But even these firms generally require financial resources which are beyond the reach of the private inventor working in his own backyard.

The amount of research and development carried out in industry has risen from $2,000 million in 1950 to nearly $11,000 million in 1961. But these figures conceal three important qualifications. First, most of industry's research effort is concerned with 'applied research' – advancing new scientific knowledge with specific commercial objectives – and even more with 'development' – the translation of research findings into actual products and processes; the latter accounts for at least three quarters of industry's research expenditure. Only a few companies in a few industries spend significant sums on 'basic research', which is usually defined as a pioneering quest for new knowledge that is not directed towards a specific technological application. Most of the nation's basic research is carried out in universities and other non-profit institutions. If private industry is to make the best and quickest use of new scientific knowledge, there must be close contact between corporate and academic research laboratories, but this does not always occur. Because of its neglect of basic research, American industry is sometimes said to be living on its intellectual capital. 'Despite all we hear to the contrary,' Dr James Killian, chairman of the Massachusetts Institute of Technology, has said, 'we have not yet created the incentives and conditions in this country which would lead to a deep penetration of research and development into our industrial community.'

The second qualification is that research and development expenditures are concentrated in a few sectors of the economy. This is illustrated in Table 7. The three leading industries – aerospace, electrical equipment and communications (including computers and electronics), chemicals and allied products – account for nearly 70 per cent of the total. It has been estimated that 80 per cent of the nation's R. and D. scientists and engineers are employed by the 350 largest corporations which account for only 60 per cent of gross national sales. Many of the low-research industries are characterized by small firms which lack the resources to undertake scientific research, but others consist of large firms which may lack a research tradition of their own, or rely (like the railway companies) on their suppliers for innovations. It does not always follow that a sharp increase in research expenditures by these industries would lead to significant improvements in productivity, but the existing distribution of research is almost certainly far short of the optimum.

Thirdly, a large part of the cost of the increased research programmes has been borne, not by industry itself, but by the Federal

TABLE 7

Research and development in industry 1961
(millions of dollars)

Industry	Total	Financed by companies	Financed by Government
Aircraft and missiles	3,957	392	3,565
Electrical equipment and communications	2,404	871	1,533
Chemicals	1,073	877	196
Machinery	896	610	286
Motor vehicles	802	628	174
Scientific instruments	384	212	172
Petroleum	294	286	8
Primary metals	160	151	9
Rubber products	126	88	38
Fabricated metal products	118	90	28
Food and kindred products	105	105	—
Stone, clay, and glass products	103	95	8
Paper and allied products	60	60	—
Textile and apparel	33	33	—
Lumber and wood products	9	9	—
Other industries	348	127	221
Total	10,872	4,631	6,241

Government. Less than 40 per cent of all the research carried out in the United States today is financed by private industry, compared with 70 per cent in 1930. As Table 8 shows, the Federal Government, which financed only 16 per cent of the total in 1930, now finances over 60 per cent. The actual performance of research is distributed in much the same manner as before between industry (74 per cent), universities and non-profit institutions (12 per cent), and Government-owned laboratories (14 per cent), but industry's dependence on the Federal Government for the bulk of its research funds has created a new situation in which the traditional incentives for industrial research – the spur of competition and the desire for profit – are no longer dominant. The bulk of the Government's support for research and development is concentrated in areas related to defence and space, and hence

TABLE 8

Expenditure on research and development 1930–59
(millions of dollars)

	1930	1953	1959
Government	23	2,810	7,200
Business firms	116	2,370	4,500
Universities	27	220	300
Total	166	5,400	12,000

in two industries – aerospace and electrical equipment and communications. Whereas the aerospace industry derives 90 per cent of its research and development funds from the Government, the chemical industry gets only 20 per cent of its research funds from the Government.

But although the expenditure of public funds for research is concentrated in a few industries, the very size of the Federal Government's research effort has had far-reaching consequences. 'The Federal Government is no longer simply aiding science and technology, it is guiding them. American science and technology are dependent on governmental action, just as American agriculture has been for many years.'[2] This situation has come about, not through any deliberate plan, but rather by accident, as the Government responded pragmatically to unexpected developments – the Second World War, the Cold War, space exploration. But now that it has come about, there is concern in the United States to ensure that the Government conducts its research activities in a way that will be of most benefit to the nation as a whole and will facilitate the advance of industrial technology.

While the scale of the Federal Government's involvement with research is a recent development, its concern with science and technology has a long history. The Constitution of 1787 gave Congress the power 'to promote the progress of science and useful arts' through the patent system, which gave inventors a seventeen-year monopoly of their inventions, and this was soon supplemented by the use of public funds to promote research in such fields as medicine and agriculture.

At a time when the bulk of the population drew their livelihood from farming, it was not surprising that the first organized Government assistance to technology should have been made in this industry. In 1862 Congress passed the Morrill Land-Grant College Act, which encouraged agricultural education, and created the Department of Agriculture to 'acquire and diffuse among the people of the United States useful information on subjects connected with agriculture'. In 1887 Congress provided for the establishment of agricultural experimental stations in each state. Thus the Government assumed partial responsibility for financing agricultural research and for disseminating its results; it created a bridge from laboratory to farm. Though this has been supplemented by the research carried out by companies which supply feed, equipment, and other materials to farmers, it is the Government which is chiefly responsible both for the efficiency of American farmers and for the embarrassingly large surpluses that have resulted from it.

Over the years, the Government has been willing to finance scientific research which it regards as essential to the public welfare, but which is too expensive, too complicated, or too uncertain of success to interest private industry. There is little pattern or logic in the Government's research activities; it assists research in air transport, but not in rail transport – it does not accept responsibility for research in transport as a whole. In many cases the dividing line between private and public responsibility is vague; private industry sometimes objects to Government research programmes which might compete with its own operations. The Government, for its part, is generally eager to hand over a new technology, such as nuclear power for electricity generation, to private industry as soon as its commercial attractiveness is demonstrated.

Some steps have been taken to coordinate the Government's research activities and to prevent unnecessary duplication. In

1950 the National Science Foundation was created as a general purpose agency 'to develop a national policy for the promotion of basic research and education in the sciences'. The N.S.F. supports basic research through scholarships and grants to the universities, operates four national research centres chiefly concerned with astronomy and atmospheric research, and acts as a clearing house of information on the employment of scientists and on the research activities of Government, industry and university. The President of the United States is assisted in the formulation of scientific policy by a Science Advisory Committee and by the Federal Council for Science and Technology, which consists of the chief scientific officers of the Government agencies mainly concerned with research. There have been suggestions that effective coordination can only be achieved through a Cabinet-level Department of Science and Technology, comparable to Britain's newly created Ministry of Technology.

But most of the Government's research activity reflects, not a general concern with science and technology, but the desire to further specific national objectives. Some 90 per cent of the Federal Government's commitment to R. and D. is directed to three purposes – the public health, national defence, and the exploration of space.

The Defence and Space Programmes

The extent to which the private economy benefits from the Government's space and defence programmes has long been a matter of dispute. The size of the Government's defence effort, accounting for about half the Federal budget and nearly 10 per cent of the nation's total production, has inevitably distorted the economy and deprived it of resources that could have been devoted to peaceful and productive purposes. There is evidence that the growth of defence R. and D., by bidding up salaries and taking the cream of scientific and engineering graduates, may have tended to reduce the quality and quantity of research done in civilian laboratories.

It is true that the civilian economy receives some 'fall-out' as a result of scientific advances made in the defence programme. Synthetic rubber, nuclear power, electronic computers, numerical control for machine tools – these are some of the new products and techniques which have been stimulated, directly or indirectly, by expenditure on defence. General Electric recently announced that it had converted a 'space age' component – a silicon-controlled rectifier–for use in domestic products like cars and toasters; it would provide the capacity to control speed, heat, and light in infinite degrees. The space programme, too, has already prepared the way for communications by satellite, and may lead to significant advances in such fields as weather forecasting, power sources, and metallurgy. But quite apart from the possibility that some of these civilian advances could have been obtained more cheaply if they had been sought directly, rather than as a by-product of defence and space programmes, it is possible that the value of 'fall-out', at least in terms of specific products and processes, will diminish in the future.

The technology of the space-defence industry has been growing steadily separate from the technology of civilian industry since the Second World War. It is partly because the requirements of cost and performance are so different that defence contractors have found it difficult to develop civilian markets. The recent drop in defence spending, which is not fully offset by the continuing rise in space expenditure, has increased the pressure for diversification among these companies, but they have mostly been unsuccessful.[3] (The few examples of successful adaptation suggest that, given adequate long-term planning and market research, the necessary adjustments can be made. It is worth noting that the task of adjustment to a lower level of defence business is left almost entirely to the companies; the Government accepts no responsibility for preserving individual companies, however important they may have been as government contractors.) There appears to be too little mobility among scientists between defence and non-defence establishments. The Federal Government, of course, actively seeks civilian outlets for its research discoveries. The National Aeronautics and Space Administration, which has found Congress increasingly reluctant to provide unlimited funds for space exploration, has stressed the importance of 'fall-out' as an argument for supporting a large space programme. But these arguments are treated with some scepticism.

It is often pointed out that, while the concentration of effort on defence and space may be regrettable, the nation's total research expenditure would be much smaller were it not for these Government programmes, and the national economy as a whole has benefited from them. According to this view, the sources of funds and the direction of research are less important than that a high level of research should be maintained. The defence and space programmes have certainly given a fillip to scientifically-oriented companies and industries that might not otherwise have had a base on which to grow; and though they may at first be concerned primarily with Government contracts, they gradually move into other fields.

The Federal Government has sometimes played a catalytic role in the development of the 'scientific complex',[4] which is potentially one of the most effective instruments for bridging the gap between academic and industrial research. The most famous of these complexes are in Boston, Massachusetts, and Palo Alto, California. In the former a large number of science-based firms has gathered round a group of outstanding universities (principally Harvard and M.I.T.) and government establishments s uch as the Air Force's Cambridge Research Laboratories and the Lincoln Laboratory. The Government has awarded research contracts both to the universities and to the science-based firms. The result is the creation of a scientific community in which discoveries made in the university or at the Government laboratory are quickly translated into industrial use. Many graduates of Harvard and M.I.T. have formed their own companies in the vicinity, drawing on the work performed in the universities; many faculty members serve as consultants to industry or on the boards of local companies. Some 400 firms, including such well-known names as Polaroid and Raytheon, have their headquarters in the area.

The formation of the Hewlett–Packard Company, now one of the world's largest manufacturers of electronic measuring instruments, illustrates the 'breeding' process which occurs in a scientific community of this kind. Both William Hewlett and David Packard were engineering students at Stanford University in California and were encouraged by their professor, Frederick Terman, to pursue certain new concepts in radio engineering; a partnership started in an old garage with a capital of $538 and a pilot oscillator blossomed into a substantial international business.

The failure rate among these new science-based companies tends to be high, because the individuals who start them sometimes have difficulty in marketing their products and hence in obtaining the necessary finance. But once a few companies like Hewlett–Packard get established, 'they create an entrepreneurial culture in which other young men are stimulated to try to develop other new firms'.[4] Government research contracts, awarded on the basis of the individuals' talent rather than the size of the organization, can help to sustain them during the early years of development.

The cross-fertilization between university and industry, which is a crucial factor in technological advance, can clearly be facilitated by the injection of Government funds. Although the Government contracts may be concerned with specific objectives in defence or space exploration, they may lead to fundamental scientific discoveries which have commercial applications. Government funds are not always essential – sometimes just the two elements, science-based firms and advanced technological universities, are sufficient to start the breeding process – but they are usually helpful.

Many American communities are trying to develop the same sort of scientific complex which has been so successful in Boston and Palo Alto. A major part of their effort is usually directed towards the Federal Government, in the hope that a major research installation, perhaps in connexion with the space programme, can be attracted to their city. Thus the Government's decisions on space and defence research can be used to facilitate scientific and technological advance in general. But it is probable that, if the Government was able to put the same degree of effort into civilian technology as into defence and space, the resulting 'scientific community' would be even more productive in terms of industrial progress and economic growth.

Others argue that the most important form of 'fall-out' from the defence and space programmes is the development of new managerial techniques for tackling large and complex problems.

Many of the most spectacular technological attainments of all time [according to a Defence Department official] have been made in the last few years through the process of deciding to undertake the projects and then organizing and funding them as necessary to get them done. The technique of organizing and directing vast team efforts on an inter-disciplinary, multi-industry basis has emerged as a new power, a new social instrument, out of the military and space programs of the past two decades.

Sometimes called 'systems engineering', it is designed for the solution, often on a 'crash' basis, of very large-scale problems, such as the construction of a supersonic airliner or the landing of a man on the moon. In civilian industry, the Bell System has consciously applied the systems approach to the problem of communications – with spectacular success. Whether the same technique can be applied on a national basis to such fields as housing and transportation, as some believe, is doubtful in view of the institutional obstacles – the multiplicity of state and local governments, the relative weakness of the Federal Government (in comparison with its accepted responsibility for national defence) – which stand in the way of effective managerial control.

It may well be that the provision of housing and transportation – two problem areas in the American economy – would be revolutionized if they were subjected to the same systematic application of material resources and managerial effort that went into the production of the atomic bomb. But there is little evidence at present that the American people would permit the nation's resources to be used in this way or approve of the extension of Federal authority that would inevitably occur. (It is possible that the Northeast Corridor Project, in which the Government is financing research into the feasibility of high-speed passenger trains between Boston, New York and Washington, could eventually involve the application of the systems approach to a large-scale civilian problem, but this programme is still at an early stage.[5] If defence spending continues to decline, attempts may be made to transfer established research and development teams to civilian problems; a start in this direction has been made on a local basis by the State of California, using the 'systems engineering' skills of defence contractors to study state problems.

Sources of Technological Advance

Whatever the exact nature of the civilian 'fall-out' from the space and defence programmes, it cannot be relied on to generate the kind of technological advance which the economy needs. Can the company-financed research programmes of private industry be relied on to fulfil the nation's objectives? There are some grounds for supposing that industry's research effort is not enough, and that either industry, or the Federal Government, or both, will have to take steps to increase support for scientific research if the nation's economic growth is to be accelerated.

The burden of industrial research is carried by a few industries. There is a wide gulf between the research-intensive industries such as electronics, chemicals and aerospace on the one hand, and low-research industries like textiles, machine tools, metal fabrication and building on the other. The leading companies in the first three industries devote a high proportion of their sales to research; within their research budgets basic research represents a significant part of the total. The value of basic research to a company depends to a large extent on its range of products. If the range is wide, covering a number of different technologies, then it is likely to benefit from a high level of spending on basic research. But even the biggest firms like General Electric and Du Pont devote far more effort to applied than to basic research. The social benefits to be derived from basic research are often much greater than the benefits that can be obtained by an individual firm, even as large and diversified a firm as General Electric. Hence there is a strong case for Federal support of basic research; this is already provided to the universities through the National Science Foundation and other agencies, but it should probably be expanded.

Even the basic research carried out at most large companies is related directly or indirectly to their business activities. Though Bell Laboratories claim to make no distinction between 'science' and 'science that is relevant to our business', its research activities are obviously related to the parent company's business of communications. Fortunately the field of communications is so wide, and the parent company's resources so great, that scope is provided for very wide-ranging and fundamental scientific research. The discovery of the transistor in 1948 is one of Bell Laboratories' most outstanding accomplishments, and in this the company acted almost as a public-spirited sponsor of innovation, creating a new industry – the semi-conductor industry – by making available to other companies the results of its own research. Although the transistor was to be of great importance in its own telephone business, the immediate application of the invention was in an industry with which the Bell System was not directly concerned.

More often a discovery has an immediate impact on the company's business; Du Pont, for example, is unlikely to have discovered nylon if it had not already been in the rayon business. The line between basic and applied research is vague, and even though these research-intensive industries may not undertake as much basic research as society, ideally, would like, their research efforts can lead to striking technological breakthroughs which they attempt to exploit, either in their own organization or by licensing the invention to others.

Some companies are less concerned with an established business than with exploiting whatever discoveries are made in their research laboratories. The company headquarters consists essentially of a central research organization which spawns new companies or even new industries. 'Its central characteristic is that it sees the company as a resource for exploiting the business potential of the new technology uncovered rather than seeing the research and development activity as a resource for improving the company's position in the business it is already in.'[6] General Electric is perhaps the most diversified research organization in the world, with a strong stake in physics, mathematics, chemistry, electronics and the aerospace sciences;[7] it is looking for new knowledge in all these fields and is prepared to exploit it, even if it involves moving away from its traditional activities and invading a new industry.

The aerospace companies are beginning to move in the same direction. Instead of being primarily concerned in the production of aircraft and missile 'hardware', firms like Lockheed and North American Aviation are transforming themselves into centres of innovation and research, still capable of producing whatever hardware is required, but with their strength in scientific excellence. Their survival both as government contractors and as businesses is seen to depend on a high level of basic research.

As these science-based companies enlarge their activities, they often find themselves in the territory of the low-research industries. The introduction of synthetic fibres by the chemical industry into the textile industry is one example of such invasion. The textile companies themselves, being mostly small and not research-conscious, originated few inventions of their own, but a number of important innovations – Sanforizing, imitation fur, stretch garments, urethane foam – were introduced by outsiders.

Similarly, the machine-tool industry consisted predominantly of small, family-owned companies, deeply committed to traditional ways of doing business and conducting little research of their own. The most important recent innovation in the industry – the use of numerical control for machine tools – stemmed in large part from research carried out by the Air Force and M.I.T. into ways of machining complex helicopter rotors. The technique spread gradually from the aerospace industry into the machine-tool industry itself, but the machine-tool makers were slow to adopt it and slow to recognize the inroads that were being made into their business by the aerospace and electronics companies. A few large firms, such as Cincinnati Milling Machines, undertook substantial research of their own, but the reaction to the invasion was generally passive.

In the building industry the introduction of new materials, like plastics, prestressed concrete and aluminium, and the new technique of treating construction as a manufacturing process, involving prefabrication of components and flow-line production, provided another illustration of the invasion process. The fragmented structure of the building industry was peculiarly unsuitable to the new processes, and for this reason resistance to change has been strong. But gradually modernization of the industry is taking place.

The invasion of one industry by another is one of the most important ways in which scientific advance is diffused.

The total process of technical innovation in American industry in recent years has consisted in the emergence of certain technically advanced industrial areas – chemistry (much but not all of this invasion has consisted in replacement of natural by synthetic products), the broad area of electronics, and aerospace – which have exerted pressures for change on traditional industry, either by serving as technological models, by making new demands on traditional industries as suppliers, or by exploiting market opportunities represented by traditional areas. Pressures for growth and expansion, as well as the interdependence of industries as sources of supply and as markets, have caused these advance waves of technology to spread out over all of industry.[8]

Just as the Federal Government is often urged to enlarge its support of basic research, so there have been suggestions that the Government should attempt to stimulate applied research in 'backward' industries, like building and machine tools. It is possible that the structure of these industries may be changed by economic forces (as, for example, in textiles, where a small number of large and diversified concerns, conscious of research and able to afford it, are beginning to emerge) so that Government intervention is not needed; or the invasion process may transform a backward industry in the required direction. But some believe that these natural processes will not work fast enough.

Thus in 1963 the Kennedy Administration proposed a civilian industrial technology programme, modelled on the agricultural extension service and designed, among other things, 'to generate the technical work not called forth in sufficient quantity by the profit incentive alone, but necessary for the technological advancement of an industry or industry segment' which was not able to support an efficient research programme of its own. Federal funds would be provided for the training of personnel at universities, for research into the industry's problems at universities and engineering schools, and for the diffusion of the latest information among the firms in the industry.

The reaction of Congress was unenthusiastic, but a limited programme was approved and some public funds have been made available for research in the laggard industries. Further investigation is being conducted into ways of assisting these industries – and into ways in which the industries can help themselves; cooperative research associations, for example, may be the vehicle for further governmental assistance. The lack of technical progress in the building industry is of special concern to the Administration, because of the tendency for costs and prices in this field to rise faster than productivity.

As the Federal Government takes a more active part in promoting economic growth, it is likely to become more closely involved in the advancement of science, in industry and in the universities, as well as for its own governmental purposes. It is recognized that the advance of scientific knowledge and its application to production is one of the key factors which determine a nation's rate of economic growth. As yet, however, there is considerable uncertainty about how much money should be spent on research, how the Government can most efficiently support research, and how innovations can be more rapidly diffused through industry. A further period of experimentation is likely to take place before final answers to these questions can be obtained.

A somewhat similar state of uncertainty exists in private industry both about the amount of research that a company should undertake and about how it should be organized.

Although the volume of company-financed research is still rising, there appears to have been some disillusionment in the last few years; the returns from research expenditure, in some cases, have been meagre. As for the organization of research, no firm conclusions have been reached. The accidental nature of many important inventions has made many firms reluctant to be dogmatic about the best way of administering a research group. I.B.M.'s disk memory unit, the heart of the random access computer, is said to have been developed as a bootleg project after the management had ruled that budget considerations required its termination.

The research vice-president of Eastman Kodak once said:

> The best person to decide what research shall be done is the man who is doing the research. The next best is the head of the department. After that you leave the field of best persons and meet increasingly worse groups. The first of these is the research director, who is probably wrong more than half the time. Then comes a committee, which is wrong most of the time. Finally, there is a committee of company vice-presidents, which is wrong all of the time.

In very few companies, however, is the freedom of the individual research worker as great as it seems to be in Bell Laboratories. Most companies have limited research budgets which they have to apportion between rival projects; the choice between the projects still involves a considerable amount of guesswork. Strenuous efforts are being made to find ways of measuring and increasing the productivity of research expenditure. In view of the trend towards shorter life-cycles for new products and processes, the effective management of research and development is likely to become one of the crucial factors in business success.

10 · Businessmen and Economic Growth

America's Economic Problems

THE United States, like other industrial countries, wants to achieve full employment without inflation and a faster rate of economic growth. The fulfilment of these objectives requires coordinated action by government and by business. The government, through its spending and taxing policies, through its support of education and health, and in many other ways, is able to influence the performance of the economy and the speed at which it grows. But the bulk of the nation's resources are controlled and managed by private individuals and companies. Their decisions, while affected by government actions, are not usually determined by them. In a country where private businessmen enjoy substantial freedom of action, faster economic growth cannot be brought about by government fiat.

The Federal Government has always been concerned directly or indirectly with economic growth. In the nineteenth century its support for agriculture and its assistance to railways and canal construction were examples of the use of public funds to increase prosperity and raise the nation's standard of living. But in the past twenty years the nation's economic objectives have become more explicit, and the Government's responsibilities in fulfilling them have been made more formal. The Employment Act of 1946 committed the Government 'to promote maximum employment, production and purchasing power', and established the Council of Economic Advisers to assist the President in the formulation of economic policies. The Joint Economic Committee of Congress, which has had a considerable influence on Government policy, was also created at that time. (These two institutions, which have no counterparts in Britain, have played an important part in raising the level of debate about economic issues both in Government and in the country at large.) Memories of mass unemployment in the 1930s facilitated a widespread, though by no means unanimous, acceptance of the view that the central government should take a more active role in promoting prosperity.

The Employment Act was an important step forward. But for the first decade or so after the war the performance of the economy did not suggest that anything more would be needed. Instead of the postwar slump that many had feared, the pent-up demand for consumer goods like houses, cars and washing machines, the need to replace ageing capital equipment that had lasted throughout the Depression and the war, the rise of science-based industries spawned by the war effort – all this paved the way for a remarkable and virtually uninterrupted ten-year boom. But after the middle of the 1950s the impetus of these new forces seemed to be spent. The rate of growth in production began to slow down, and unemployment rose. Manufacturers' output rose by an average of 4·3 per cent a year in the 1947–57 period, but by only 3·3 per cent in 1957–62. While unemployment averaged 4·2 per cent of the civilian labour force in the first postwar decade, and fell as low as 2·9 per cent in 1953, the average between the winter of 1957 and the winter of 1965 was 5·7 per cent.

It was also noted that the last period in which reasonably full employment was achieved – between 1955 and 1957 – was accompanied by a very sharp rise in wages and prices which had the effect of weakening the nation's ability to compete in world markets; America's share in world exports of manufactured goods fell significantly between 1956 and 1958. In the following six years, when unemployment was high, prices and wages rose much more slowly. Indeed, between 1957 and 1962 unit labour costs in the U.S. rose by only 1 per cent, compared with 14 per cent in Japan, 17 per cent in the U.K. and 26 per cent in West Germany. This seemed to pose an unpleasant choice between high unemployment and stable prices on the one hand, and full employment and inflation on the other. A new combination of public and private policies was sought which would provide an answer to this dilemma.

An added reason for concern was the recognition that other countries, including the Soviet Union, were growing much more rapidly than the United States in the 1950s. This is illustrated in

Table 9. While the standard of living in most of these countries was still far below that of the United States, their apparent ability to sustain a high rate of growth and full employment was a cause for envy and concern.

TABLE 9

International growth rates 1950–60
(annual average rate of increase, per cent)

Japan	8·8
Germany	7·5
U.S.S.R.	6·8
Italy	5·9
France	4·3
U.S.A.	3·3
U.K.	2·6

At first their higher rate of growth was ascribed to the effect of postwar recovery, but their consistently superior performance in the later 1950s threw doubt on this explanation. There was a suspicion that other countries had found methods of stimulating growth which were not being used by the U.S. It was felt that, unless America's economy performed at least as well as the economies of other countries, her position of world leadership would be threatened. She would be unable to afford the large programmes of military and economic aid to the developing countries without excessive strain on her domestic resources.

The commitment to faster economic growth was formally expressed in 1961, when the United States joined with the other nineteen member-nations of the Organization for Economic Cooperation and Development in setting as a target the attainment of a 50 per cent (4·1 per cent a year) increase in their combined real gross national products over the decade from 1960 to 1970. This required a very considerable improvement on America's performance in the 1953–60 period, when the average annual rise was only 2·4 per cent.

A further cause for anxiety about the performance of the American economy was the persistence of a large balance-of-payments deficit. The United States had been running deficits in its international accounts since 1950, but in the late 1950s and the early 1960s the deficits became larger and more alarming. There was still a substantial surplus of exports over imports, despite the drop in America's share of world trade, but the surplus was not enough to offset the outflow of funds, both public and private, for other purposes. The Federal Government was spending large sums abroad on military and economic aid, and although part of this aid was 'tied' to American goods, the net capital outflow was considerable. Private individuals and companies were investing large sums in foreign countries, by building or acquiring manufacturing plants overseas, and by buying the shares of foreign companies. American banks were lending on a big scale to foreign governments and companies. The surplus on current account was not large enough to cover the increase in long-term investment overseas and in short-term lending to foreigners. The deficit was financed partly by an increase in America's liquid liabilities to foreigners, partly by the sale of gold; the U.S. gold stock fell from $22,000 million in 1955 to $14,000 million in 1965.

In the earlier postwar period the outflow of dollars was welcomed by foreign countries, which needed to replenish their reserves of gold and foreign exchange; they could either keep the dollars in their reserves or transfer them into gold by selling them to the U.S. Treasury. But in recent years the outflow of dollars has become excessive; partly through fear of a possible devaluation, foreign countries were reluctant to hold large dollar balances and converted a bigger proportion into gold, thus imposing a strain on American gold reserves. The United States has been obliged to look for ways of cutting and, if possible, eliminating its balance-of-payments deficit, either by increasing its trade surplus or by reducing the outflow of public and private capital.

The Need for Cooperation

This was the context in which President Kennedy took office in 1961. The state of the economy was sufficiently unsatisfactory to call for vigorous action by the Government on a number of fronts. On the domestic front, the immediate need was to reduce the level of unemployment, which at that time was close to 7 per cent. The Kennedy Administration set as its interim target the achievement of a 4 per cent rate of unemployment, which would correspond to a British rate of about 2·7 per cent. It is worth emphasizing that the high American unemployment rate of recent years is not, as is sometimes supposed, a statistical illusion. It is true that the American figures are based on sample surveys, while European figures are generally based on registrations at labour exchanges or records of unemployment insurance payments. To be comparable, the British rate has to be raised by about a half or the American rate reduced by about a third. But as Table 10 shows, even when the European figures are adjusted to U.S. definitions, this does not alter the relatively poor performance of the United States between 1959 and 1964.

TABLE 10

Unemployment in Europe and the U.S.A. 1959–64
(as a percentage of the labour force, adjusted to U.S. definitions)

	U.S.A.	U.K.	France	Germany
1959	5·5	3·1	2·8	1·6
1960	5·6	2·4	2·7	0·7
1961	6·7	2·3	2·4	0·4
1962	5·6	2·9	2·5	0·4
1963	5·7	3·4	3·1	0·5
1964	5·2	2·5	2·5	0·4

A 4 per cent rate might seem a modest target in view of what has been achieved in Europe, but it was always assumed that unemployment would eventually be brought well below that level. President Johnson's Secretary of Labour, Willard Wirtz, has defined full employment as lying between 2·5 and 3 per cent; this would be more in line with Britain's idea of full employment, which is usually reckoned at about 1·5 per cent in British terms. As it happened, even the interim target proved much more elusive than President Kennedy and his advisers had supposed. It was not until the beginning of 1966 that 4 per cent was finally reached.

The basic reason for the persistence of high unemployment was inadequate demand. The Government's task was no longer to restrain demand, as it had been for most of the first post-war decade, but to stimulate it. This it could do either by increasing its own expenditures or by increasing the spending power of companies and individuals through a reduction in taxes.

The choice of policies seems simple, but in practice the Government's freedom of action has been limited by a widespread American belief, held particularly in the business community, that taxes should be levied solely to cover necessary Government expenditures, no more and no less. The Federal Budget is often regarded as a test of the Government's financial prudence; if revenue does not cover expenditures, the Government is thought to be 'living beyond its means', acting as foolishly as a family which spends more than it earns; the balancing of the budget, which is almost never a political issue in Britain, is a very burning one in the U.S. It has been difficult for many Americans to accept the notion that the Government's spending and taxing powers are weapons which can be used to keep the volume of demand in line with the nation's productive capacity – that if demand appears to be outrunning capacity, spending should be reduced or taxes raised, and that if demand is inadequate, the Government should take steps to stimulate it.

The Kennedy Administration decided in 1963 that a big tax reduction for individuals and businesses was necessary to bring the economy to its full capacity. The enactment of this $11,000 million tax cut marked something of a watershed in Government policy, since it involved the acceptance of deliberate budgetary deficits over a period of several years; the argument was that a balanced budget could be achieved when the economy had reached full capacity. Many Americans were uneasy about the tax cut, feeling that it could only be justified if the Government reduced its expenditures by a corresponding amount – a step which would have nullified the economic effects of the tax cut. The opposition might well have carried the day had it not been for large-scale propaganda efforts on behalf of the tax bill carried out among private businessmen. A businessmen's committee for tax reduction was formed at the Administration's suggestion, in which the presidents of two very large companies – Ford Motor

Company and the Pennsylvania Railroad – played a leading part in overcoming the misgivings of the business community.

This was an example of one form of cooperation between businessmen and the Government to achieve objectives which both regard as desirable. It requires a consensus of opinion which has been lacking on other economic issues. It could have been argued that a better way to stimulate demand was for the Government to increase its own expenditures, and that this would not only bring the economy up to full capacity, but would also satisfy many important needs in connexion with education, hospitals, and other public facilities; the public sector of the American economy is often said to be 'starved' in relation to the private sector. But many businessmen are instinctively opposed to increases in public expenditures, and insist that the existing division of responsibilities between the public and private sectors should be preserved. President Kennedy's Council of Economic Advisers pleaded that 'if our economy is to use its productive resources in reasonable accordance with a consensus as to national priorities, we must face the question of public versus private expenditures pragmatically, in terms of intrinsic merits and costs, not in terms of fixed preconceptions'.[1] But this is an area in which no consensus has yet been reached; the fixed preconceptions of businessmen have tended to stand in the way of any programmes involving large-scale increases in Federal expenditure.

Another gap in the Government's armoury is the lack of authority to vary taxes and public expenditures with sufficient speed to cope with the sudden changes in private demand that bring inflation or recession. A major tax-cut proposal involves a delay of many months between submission to Congress and enactment. President Kennedy asked Congress for stand-by powers to alter tax and expenditure policies within certain prescribed limits. A similar request was made by President Johnson, but Congress is jealous of its powers over taxing and spending, and is reluctant to concede this new authority to the executive branch. (It is possible that if the business community became convinced of the need for greater flexibility along these lines, its support would ensure its enactment, but this has not yet occurred.)

Inflation normally occurs when demand exceeds the nation's capacity to produce. Thus in 1946-8, when consumers and businesses began buying on a massive scale to replenish the shortages caused by the war, and again in 1950-51 during the Korean War, demand outran supply, and prices rose sharply. But the next inflationary period of 1955-8 could not be explained on quite the same grounds. Demand was unusually heavy in one sector of the economy – the supply of durable manufactured goods – but other important factors, in the view of the Council of Economic Advisers, were 'the use of market power by management to maintain profit margins despite rising costs, the exercise of market power by labour unions in an effort to capture a substantial share of rising profits for their membership, and the transmission of these developments to other sectors of the economy'.[2] Private companies and unions are seen to have a freedom of action, independent of the pressure of demand in the economy, which can be used to the detriment of price stability.

The problem could conceivably be tackled by a forceful application of the antitrust laws to both companies and unions, so that market power itself would be eliminated. But this would involve so drastic a change in the institutional structure of the economy as to be hardly practicable. Instead, the existence of some degree of market power is recognized as inevitable, and other methods are devised to ensure that market power will be used consistently with the public interest. In Britain the Labour Government approached the problem through the 'incomes policy' and the establishment of the Prices and Incomes Board. The United States has tried to develop what the Council has called 'a national policy to enlist the force of public opinion to maintain cost–price stability'.

In 1961 President Kennedy's Council of Economic Advisers formulated 'guideposts' which were designed to set standards for non-inflationary price and wage behaviour. The Council said, in effect, that wage increases (including fringe benefits) in a particular firm or industry should not exceed the annual increase in 'national trend output per man-hour'.[3] The standard was not the productivity trend in the particular firm or industry, nor the particular year's increase in productivity, which might be affected by short-run factors. The key figure was the average rise in productivity in the economy as a whole over a period of several recent years. Since 1960 the growth in productivity has averaged about 3·2 per cent a year in the private economy.

As for prices, the Council said that if an industry's 'trend productivity' is growing less rapidly than the national trend, prices can be raised enough to cover the increase in its labour costs – assuming that wages have risen in line with the national productivity trend. If an industry's productivity is rising faster than the national average, so that its labour costs per unit of output are actually falling, then prices should be cut. As the Council put it, 'in a world where large firms and large unions play an essential role, the cost–price record will depend heavily upon the responsibility with which they exercise the market power that society entrusts to them'.

The guideposts are purely voluntary. Their effectiveness depends on the willingness of the Administration, especially the President himself, to press for their acceptance, and on the willingness of companies and unions to abide by them. As to the first, both President Kennedy and President Johnson frequently referred to the guideposts in appealing for responsible action on wages and prices. The chairman of President Kennedy's Council of Economic Advisers, Walter Heller, was outspoken in criticizing particular decisions. Under the Council's guidance, the Administration took steps 'to follow emerging price and wage developments with great care and to assemble data which will illuminate the price- and wage-making situations in particular industries'.[4] The report on steel in the summer of 1965* was designed to influence both the price situation – there had been rumours of an impending increase – and the wage negotiations which were then in progress.

The effectiveness of the guideposts has not yet been fully tested. Between 1960 and 1964 the average rise in earnings (including

*See page 41.

fringe benefits) was about 3·3 per cent a year in manufacturing and 3·6 per cent in the economy as a whole – just about in line with the guideposts. This performance compares favourably with the experience of earlier periods of expansion in the post-war period, notably the expansion of 1955–7 when wages rose much faster than productivity. But the real test for the guideposts will come during a period of full employment. The context for the introduction of America's version of an incomes policy in 1961 was in complete contrast to the situation in Britain in 1964, when the Labour Government established a rather similar 'norm' of 3–3½ per cent for incomes. Britain was facing a situation of severe labour scarcity, which was pushing up prices and wages at an alarming rate; it seemed unlikely that the incomes policy could ever get off the ground until the pressure of demand had eased; the deflationary measures of 1965 were designed to have this effect. In the United States, on the other hand, there were no serious capacity bottlenecks or manpower shortages.

Even in conditions of high unemployment there were some disturbing breaches in the guideposts. The wage settlement in the motor industry in 1964 involved a 4·9 per cent increase in labour costs. The Council of Economic Advisers felt that this settlement would have been much smaller if the manufacturers had adhered to the price guidepost; productivity in the industry, in the Council's view, was rising faster than the national average, and price reductions were called for. The advice was not taken and in its annual report for 1965 the Council criticized the industry's 'unusually high profits' which served as inviting targets for inflationary wage increases. As the pressure of demand for labour and materials, aggravated by the Vietnam war, intensified, President Johnson and his advisers began to intervene more forcefully in industries, such as construction, where the trend of costs and prices was clearly in excess of the guideposts.

The guideposts were strongly attacked by some businessmen and economists, who felt that the Administration had no right to interfere in the price and wage decisions of private industry. Arthur Burns, who had been chairman of President Eisenhower's Council of Economic Advisers, argued that the guideposts would throttle competition and act as a drag on efficiency. But others agreed with the Administration that the traditional measures for curbing inflation – the use of government fiscal and monetary policy to regulate the amount of demand in the economy, and the use of antitrust weapons to increase the forces of competition – needed to be supplemented by some form of restraint on the 'market power' of large unions and companies.

The Council itself was convinced that the guideposts had helped to create a new climate of opinion.

Many groups in our society [the Council said in its 1965 Report] now have a better understanding of the relationships between costs and prices. There is increasing realization that it is appropriate – indeed necessary – to consider whether a proposed course of action, if followed by others in similar circumstances, would be consistent with over-all stability. Decision-makers in unions and managements are increasingly aware both of the fact that their decisions affect the public interest and of the fact that the public is interested in their decisions.

A cooperative approach has also been attempted in tackling the balance-of-payments problem. Here, too, both parties agree that the deficit must be eliminated, but businessmen have tended to demand sharp cuts in Government overseas expenditure, while the Government has looked for ways of curbing private capital outflows. In 1964 the Government did impose a restriction on portfolio investment through the interest-equalization tax, which raised the cost of borrowing by foreigners in the United States; the tax virtually put a stop to the raising of capital in New York by foreign borrowers, which had been a major source of capital outflows. But this did not affect the outflow of capital that stemmed from the 'internationalization' of business – the investment by U.S. companies in overseas manufacturing facilities.

This could also have been stopped by decree, or discouraged by a tax. But President Johnson, who enjoyed an unusually good relationship with the business community, preferred a voluntary approach. He obtained the cooperation of some 500 large firms which did more than $10 million of overseas business a year or which had foreign investments worth more than $10 million, and persuaded them to make voluntary reports to the Secretary of Commerce, on a quarterly basis, on their individual balances of payments. They were urged to seek ways of minimizing the outflow of capital by making greater use of local sources of finance and always to take account of the national objective of balance-of-payments equilibrium.

'I am asking you', the President told businessmen, 'to join hands with me in a voluntary partnership. I am asking you to show the world that an aroused and responsible business community can close ranks and make a voluntary program work'. The programme was later extended to include more detailed targets for capital outflows and bank lending. It clearly went a good deal further than the familiar appeals for business cooperation, and it was a remarkable example of the willingness of the business community to accept voluntarily restrictions on their freedom of action for the sake of the national interest. There were, of course, other ways in which businessmen could help in solving the balance-of-payments problem, notably by increasing their exports, and the Government provided financial incentives, as well as encouragement, for the export drive. But the voluntary machinery for controlling capital outflows was a novel experiment in Government–business cooperation.

Some businessmen were appalled by this trend towards cooperation. The chairman of the Chase Manhattan Bank alleged that the new practice of 'government by guideline' represented 'a giant step in the direction towards Federal domination of the economy'. He was angered by the balance-of-payments guidelines, which had a severe impact on his own company's operations, but he also complained bitterly of 'guidelines for wages and prices, guidelines for labour–management behaviour, guidelines for antitrust enforcement, guidelines for television advertising, even guidelines on how much you put in the collection plate on Sunday'. It was, he said, one of the most insidious and dangerous developments on the national scene. Although these remarks may have struck an answering chord in the hearts of some businessmen, there was very little evidence of any refusal to cooperate. Partly because of President Johnson's uncanny ability to win the support of conservative businessmen for apparently radical proposals, partly because influential businessmen recognize the need for such proposals, the trend towards cooperation seems likely to continue. It was significant that the reaction of businessmen to President Johnson's clash with the aluminium companies in 1965 was very much milder than it had been after President Kennedy's battle with U.S. Steel in 1962. The more active, interventionist policy on the part of the Federal Government, which had started under President Kennedy, was coming to be accepted.

Long-term Objectives

How can businessmen contribute to the long-term objective of a faster rate of economic growth? A nation's growth rate is determined primarily by the growth rate of the labour force and by the growth rate of average output per worker. As to the former, the United States is now benefiting from the high postwar birth rates. During the 1960s the labour force is expected to grow by about 1·7 per cent a year, compared to only 1·2 per cent a year in the 1950s. This creates a problem in that demand has to grow fast enough to accommodate the new supply of workers, but it also provides an opportunity for increasing the growth rate. The supply of labour can be influenced in certain directions by public policy; immigration laws, for example, can be liberalized to permit a larger inflow of foreigners. But the most important source of growth, and the one most susceptible to public policy, is the rise in average output per worker. If the labour force grows by 1·7 per cent a year and output per worker by 2·3 per cent a year (which is about the average postwar rate), total output would grow by 4 per cent a year. To raise the growth rate to 4·5 per cent a year would require an increase in the growth of productivity from 2·3 per cent to 2·8 per cent.

Recent studies suggest that the most important single factor in economic growth is the rise in the educational level of the labour force; it seems to be even more important than improved technology or increased capital investment per worker. Although the Federal Government plays a role in supporting certain vocational education, the primary and secondary schools are organized and financed by the local and state authorities. The disparity in quality of education between different states and localities, depending on the financial strength of the community, has brought pressure for Federal financial aid to secondary education. This has long been resisted on the familiar ground that it would represent an intrusion by the central government into local affairs, although in 1965 President Johnson secured the enactment of a measure providing for selective Federal aid to secondary education. The business community has generally taken a conservative position on this issue, but there are signs of a more flexible approach. For example, Thomas J. Watson, chairman of I.B.M., pointed out:

The quality of education has become a critical factor in national strength. This consideration, to my way of thinking, far outweighs any fears I might have about Federal aid to education. The important thing in a situation like this is to solve the problem and to solve it by the best means, even if this does call for some change in tradition.[5]

Business plays a more direct role in the training of adult workers which, like secondary education, represents an important investment in economic growth. Skill requirements are rising; it is estimated that employment of professional and technical workers will increase by 65 per cent between 1960 and 1975, while that of 'operatives and kindred workers' will rise by only 18 per cent.

While U.S. employers have played a significant role in upgrading the skills of the labour force, there appears to be too little cooperation between business and local educational authorities in assessing future requirements and making provision for training. Moreover, extensive training programmes are often limited to the larger companies. According to a Labour Department survey formal training is provided by less than one in five companies and is often limited to specific occupations.

Programs for the development of skills or knowledge of workers generally have been uncommon in industry except where a shortage of desired skills or levels of competence cannot be met by other means. Some firms are reluctant to invest in formal training programs because trained workers may readily move to other employers.[6]

The need for investment in training is particularly important in order to facilitate the mobility of workers from one job to another. Although American society is often regarded as the most mobile in the world, there is some evidence that the degree of labour mobility has been declining. This is partly due to the seniority systems which tie a worker to a particular firm, and to the growth of private pension schemes. Here, too, a combination of private and public policies is required. Employers and unions have developed a variety of mobility-aiding devices, including interplant seniority pools, relocation allowances, early retirement provisions, and severance-pay plans which provide a worker with a lump-sum payment as compensation for displacement. Private pension plans have in some cases been adapted to provide for the 'vesting' of pension rights on behalf of employees, so that they can carry the rights with them when they leave for other employment.

In the last few years, there has been a more active manpower policy on the Federal Government's part, supplementing the programmes of private industry. Most of the Government's activity had previously been concerned with the mitigation of hardships arising from unemployment. The Area Redevelopment Act of 1961 is mainly concerned with bringing new employment opportunities to depressed areas, and the Manpower Development and Training Act of 1962 provides training allowances for the unemployed. An O.E.C.D. report on manpower policy in the U.S. stressed the advantages of a growth-oriented policy as opposed to an unemployment-oriented policy.

Concern about future growth tends to provoke questions of training requirements, of the need for mobility of either workers or jobs, at an earlier stage than does a policy for reducing unemployment. The volume of investment in manpower development and deployment under an unemployment-oriented policy will tend to be determined by considerations of social equity. With a growth orientation it ought to reflect the expected pay-off in terms of, for example, the additional product obtained by filling vacancies, or in the long run by a given increase in, say, advanced training in mathematics.[7]

Programmes for training and retraining, for improving the mobility of labour, are ways of facilitating adjustment to technological change. There have been suggestions by some writers that 'automation' is about to bring about a massive increase in unemployment, as computer-operated machines take the place of human beings. These fears are certainly premature. Quite apart from the fact that 'automation' in the sense of controlling processes by electronic computers is still in its infancy, it is not yet clear that the technological changes involved in it are different in kind or degree from past technological improvements.

On the basis of our historical experience, automation should be recognized for what it is – an open door to a more productive economy, to higher levels of private consumption, to more effective public services, and to larger resources for the support of our international objectives.[8]

It is certainly true that mechanization and automation are reducing the demand for certain types of labour in certain industries. A survey[9] of technological trends in thirty-six major industries indicated that in eighteen of them, including coal, oil, foundries, railways, telephones and textiles, employment would decline by 1970; in seven of them, including electric power, iron and steel, motor vehicles, pulp and paper, and cigarettes, the outlook was uncertain; in the remainder, including air transport, banking, construction, electronics, insurance, printing, retail and wholesale trade, and road haulage, employment was likely to rise. These technological changes pose serious problems of job displacement and adjustment, but it is not clear that they will be any more serious than those which have occurred in the past. One of the biggest structural changes in the demand for manpower in the postwar period has been the shift from goods-producing industries towards the service trades; the proportion of workers in goods-producing industries has dropped from 51 per cent in 1947 to 40 per cent in 1963. This creates difficult problems, for the movement of workers into the low-wage, low-productivity service sector is bound to be slow. (Since 1929 real output per man in the service industries has risen by an average annual rate of 0·7 per cent, compared to 2·4 per cent in the rest of the economy.[10]) Within the goods-producing sector, too, there has been a sharp rise in the proportion of non-production workers.

There is no doubt that structural changes of this sort have contributed to the high unemployment of recent years, even though the biggest single factor has been inadequacy of demand. Hence an active manpower policy is seen as a necessary accompaniment to general measures, like tax reduction, to increase demand. Over the longer term, the connexion between manpower programmes and economic growth is more clearly recognized. Effective manpower policies, which have traditionally been concerned with alleviating the effects of unemployment, will become even more necessary as unemployment falls below 4 per cent. One of President Kennedy's major achievements was to win support for a more expansionary fiscal policy and a more positive manpower policy on the part of the Federal Government; under his Administration and that of his successor, the Government's role in promoting economic growth was decisively altered and strengthened. As one official put it:

We are threshing our way towards the European position – full employment through promotion of demand and an active manpower policy to restrain inflationary pressures by tailoring jobs to the abilities of the competitively disadvantaged, providing adequate skills, and aiding quick adjustment to any displacement.[11]

A mobile and well-trained labour force must be provided with better tools if its productivity is to grow. Skilled labour is of little use unless it has advanced machinery to work with. Better tools stem in large part from investment in research and development. Responsibility for the advance of science and technology is shared between the Government, the universities and private industry, but it is industry which is chiefly responsible for applying scientific discoveries to production, and this takes place through investment in new plant and equipment. 'Without investment in new and renewed plant and equipment, skills and inventions remain preconditions of growth; with it, they become ingredients'.[12]

Capital stock per worker, arising from industry's investment in new plant and equipment, rose by 3·5 per cent a year from 1947 to 1954, and output per worker rose by 3·3 per cent a year. In the 1954–60 period the capital stock rose by 1·9 per cent, and output per worker by only 2·1 per cent. The lag in capital investment is largely due to the inadequacy of demand; the recent steps to increase demand have helped to stimulate investment. In addition, the Government has provided special incentives, in the form of lower corporate taxes, higher allowances for depreciation, and a tax credit for new capital investment.

Despite the high standard of living, there appears to be no lack of profitable outlets for new investment. It is sometimes suggested that the American economy is reaching a stage of 'satiation', where the capacity to produce has outdistanced the capacity to consume. But the persistence of poverty on a large scale, especially among minority groups, suggests that there is still a long way to go. As living standards rise, moreover, there is a remarkable constancy in the percentage of income which is spent; since 1950 American consumers have continued to spend between 92 and 94 per cent of their disposable income on consumer goods and services. American society is not yet so affluent that it does not need a faster rate of economic growth.

Under the Administrations of President Kennedy and President Johnson faster economic growth has been explicitly recognized as an objective of public policy. This attitude is reflected in a more conscious use of existing weapons – the budget, tax policy, monetary policy – to promote economic growth, and in the development of new weapons – manpower policy, the use of public funds for research, wage–price policy – for the same purpose. The reaction of the business community has been mixed. Some observers feared that, because the relationship between business and Government was 'one of latent hostility which occasionally breaks out into rather more open warfare',[13] a deliberate growth policy would be impossible to carry through.

But there are signs that the new generation of professional businessmen is less doctrinaire and more sophisticated in its approach to economic problems. President Kennedy complained that the dialogue between business and Government 'is clogged by illusion and platitude and fails to reflect the true realities of contemporary American society'. By his actions and his measures, President Kennedy helped to dispel many of the myths – about the size of government, about the balanced budget, about the national debt – which impeded the rational and clear-headed management of the domestic economy. Under President Johnson, with his flair for winning the confidence of businessmen, a degree of consensus on some important economic issues seems to be emerging. There are important areas of conflict, notably in the field of wage–price policy, but even this emotional issue is being examined more pragmatically.

It is conceivable that in the future the cooperation between business and Government will be developed to the point where, for example, some form of long-range economic planning might be accepted. There has been considerable interest, not confined to academic circles, in the system of 'indicative planning' used in France and now being adopted by Britain. The system involves the calculation of a feasible rate of economic growth over a period of at least five years; private businessmen can make their investment plans with some degree of confidence that investments on a similar scale will be made by other industries and by the Government. In American industry internal planning within the corporation has reached a high degree of elaboration and sophistication; more re-fined long-term planning techniques are being developed which eliminate much of the old trial-and-error procedure. But a company's planning is frequently frustrated by faulty calculations of external factors, including the actions of government and of other industries. Much of this uncertainty could be removed through a cooperative attempt by business and Government to work out detailed projections of the crucial elements in the economy over a five-year period. A detailed input–output analysis of the economy, including forward-demand projections for all the major industries, can be achieved with the aid of new statistical and data-processing

181

techniques. This approach need not involve any more control by the central government than exists at present, but would simply extend the forward-planning techniques of the individual corporation to the economy as a whole. As one economist has said:

Nothing could be more futile and self-defeating than to pretend that factual analysis can supersede the traditional process of political decisions on economic matters. But it can smooth the path and thus increase the rate and reduce the costs of economic progress.[14]

It is reasonable to ascribe at least part of the improvement in America's economic performance since 1961 to the greater flexibility of Government policy and to the new developments in business–Government cooperation. It is true that full employment has taken a long time to achieve, but the rate of economic growth between 1960 and 1965, averaging 4·5 per cent a year (comfortably exceeding the 4·1 per cent target set by O.E.C.D.), has been impressive, both in relation to America's past performance and to that of European countries. In his report to Congress early in 1966 President Johnson was able to claim: 'A few years ago much was heard of the "European economic miracle". Today, across the Atlantic and around the world one hears again of the "American economic miracle"!' The challenge which America now faces is how to maintain this rate of advance – and to reduce unemployment further – without allowing the economy to boil over into inflation.

11 · Business and Society

THE businessman is concerned with getting things done. His primary function is to produce goods and services for the public, and to produce them as efficiently as possible. But his influence on society extends beyond business itself. In the United States, perhaps more than in any other country, the successful businessman has enjoyed high social prestige. His opinions and prejudices, his outlook on life, have been admired more than despised. In the absence of any effective counter-ideology, which in some other countries has been provided by the labour movement, the business ideology has tended to dominate.

The power of the modern business corporation, in its internal structure and in its relations with the outside world, has been compared to that of the medieval church. One writer describes the large corporation as the 'institutionalized expression of our way of life', while to another it is 'the institution which sets the standard for the way of life and the mode of living of our citizens; which leads, moulds, and directs; which determines our perspective on our own society; around which crystallize our social problems and to which we look for their solution'.[1]

Even if the power of the corporation is not quite as all-encompassing as these writers suggest, there is no doubt that its influence on society is greater than that of any other institution with the possible exception of the Government itself. There is also, perhaps, a tendency for some corporation managers to regard themselves as the chosen few of society, selected by their ability and training not merely to manage American business, but to give leadership to society as a whole.

Some writers have warned that 'private enterprise is only one interest within the larger fold of democratic society', and that 'the assumption of complete identity of interest may lead businessmen stealthily to the view that no one knows better than they what the community interest is, even though their vantage point is surely as much off to one angle as that of any other interested group'.[2] Many businessmen would accept this and would shy away from suggestions that they are, or should be, arbiters of the public interest. Whether they like it or not, however, it does appear that the large corporation can be held responsible for some important aspects of American society; the universities, for example, and the mass media, especially television, owe their continued existence to financial support from business corporations and are inevitably influenced by them.

This is not a sinister conspiracy to seize control of the nation. The point is simply that the outlook of the business corporation and its managers on the social issues of the day carry very great weight, and there is no evidence to suggest that their views are more enlightened than those of any other group. The Negro struggle for equality, for example, has found the business community just as unprepared and hesitant as any other section of society. It was only under strong prodding from the Federal Government that the large corporations with subsidiaries in the South used their influence in support of racial harmony; it was significant, in fact, that the local managers of the Northern-based corporations were often more reluctant to disturb the *status quo* (by a more liberal hiring policy towards Negroes, for example) than the Southern-born businessmen.

The businessman is not usually interested in politics for its own sake. He may use his influence in Congress to attain particular objectives, such as protection from competition, but he has no desire for political power itself. He is chiefly concerned with autonomy, with the freedom to manage his business as he thinks fit. But from this essentially negative posture springs the businessman's characteristic attitude to the world outside his business – his conservatism. He is inclined to fight for the *status quo*, partly through fear of the unknown, partly because his own freedom of action may be threatened by change.

As has been seen, the businessman is particularly insistent that the existing division of responsibilities between public and private institutions should not be altered in favour of the Government. He tends to fight against new programmes which involve Government expenditure, and the effect of his propaganda is that, as

J. K. Galbraith has said, 'privately produced goods and services, even of the most frivolous sort, enjoy a moral sanction not accorded to any public service except defence'.[3] According to this philosophy, any increase in public at the expense of private responsibilities will push the United States further along 'the road to serfdom'.

Perhaps the dominance of the business corporation and the business ideology is the price which America has to pay for her industrial efficiency. The United States is sometimes said to be the only country where the economy takes precedence over the other needs of society, but if it were somehow possible to 'de-economize' American society and reduce the influence of the business corporation, the performance of the economy as a whole might suffer.

What are the effects of the dominant influence of business in American society? Robert Heilbroner has criticized the business ideology of today as 'depicting a society not sufficiently different from our own to serve as a lodestar for the distant future'. He admits that the modern age hesitates before transcendental visions, and this is part of the reason for 'the unchallenged predominance of the matter of fact, conserving, incrementally progressive, and, at its best, decent and sober philosophy of the businessman'. But the question he asks is 'whether, under the thrall of such an ideology, we shall succeed in fundamentally changing a society in which most men still lead lives to which those few who have escaped would not like their sons to return'.[4]

The challenges that face American society are greater than ever before. At home the Negro revolution has imposed new pressures on the political and social fabric. By demanding improvements in their lot through organized political action, in place of (or at least in addition to) the time-honoured method of individual self-advancement, the Negroes have presented a genuinely radical challenge to the *status quo*. Although the hopes entertained by some civil rights leaders of a political union with the labour movement, to form a new 'Left', have been frustrated by the political indifference of the unions, the Negro protest has focused attention on many aspects of American life that had previously been obscured by fashionable talk of the affluent society. The persistence of extreme poverty in such areas as the Appalachian mountains, the lack of job opportunities for teenagers, the immense problem of the slums in the cities and the inadequacy of the schools – these have now become urgent public issues. The problems, moreover, are not just the loose ends of the affluent society which can easily be tidied away by the continuation of existing policies. They call for new approaches from business as well as from government, which may run counter to traditional attitudes and prejudices.

The Negro movement has a special significance for America because it is related to the 'revolution of rising expectations' which is now in progress among the poorer countries of the world. The United States, as the leader of the Western world, is deeply involved in the struggle to close the gap between rich and poor nations. Its generosity in providing aid is unquestioned, and the idealism of such ventures as the Peace Corps is much admired. But the question that has often been asked is whether America, with its emotional commitment to a certain version of 'capitalism', is capable of coming to terms with the radicalism of the nationalist movements in the developing countries. The unhappy history of relations between the United States and Latin America reflects the clash between conservative attitudes and revolutionary aspirations.

While it would be wrong to ascribe to businessmen a controlling influence over American foreign policy, business attitudes have sometimes seemed to stand in the way of rational choice. The foreign-aid programme, for example, has been inhibited by the insistence on the part of businessmen that American funds should not be used to finance government-owned projects, such as a steel mill, which would compete with private enterprise. This has encouraged the suspicion that the United States is trying to dictate to the developing countries what kind of social and economic structure they should have. The inflexibility of American attitudes towards Communist nations owes something to the inflexibility of the American business ideology.

Can the United States, a conservative country despite its

revolutionary origins, come to terms with revolution at home and abroad? The most encouraging development of the last few years has been the emergence within the business community of a rather more flexible attitude towards social and political issues. The increasingly professional approach to business problems is beginning to affect the opinions of businessmen on other issues. The closer contact between business and the academic and scientific communities is helping to widen the businessman's vision. It is possible, too, that after the buffeting of the New Deal (it is sometimes said that the business community was put on trial in the 1930s and secured its acquittal in the 1940s), businessmen have recovered their self-confidence and no longer need to adopt a defensive posture in the face of new political proposals and ideas. The views of 'progressive' businessmen on the issues of the day, as expressed by an organization like the Committee for Economic Development, are very different in tone and content from the doctrinaire free-enterprise philosophy of the past.

One of the leaders of the new school is Thomas J. Watson, chairman of I.B.M.

As businessmen [he says], we are innovators and we take pride in such things as technological improvements. Yet when it comes to social problems, we seem curiously unwilling on too many occasions to risk any kind of innovation. What makes this posture all the more ironic is that the American businessman, almost always a conservative in national affairs, is the world's champion problem-solver in his own shop. I propose again that we carry the same attitude to national affairs, where problem-solving is ever more vital.[5]

In economic affairs, as was noted in the last chapter, the rational, fact-finding, problem-solving approach has already had useful results. Instead of reacting to proposed reforms with slogans about the evils of government and the sanctity of private enterprise, businessmen are more inclined to recognize the existence of new problems and to be open-minded in their choice of solutions. This has helped to dispel many of the myths which, as President Kennedy complained, have hindered sensible management of the economy. Not only is the role of the Government viewed more pragmatically, but a more critical eye is being turned on other institutions, including the corporation itself. The apparently undemocratic nature of the corporation, and its dominant role in society, are issues which are being thoughtfully studied by businessmen as well as by their critics. A clearer understanding of the workings of the American economy is gradually emerging.

The new generation of businessmen may be able to make a more effective contribution to the discussion and solution of the nation's social and political problems. There will, of course, always be conflicting elements within American society. The need for a strong central government runs counter to the traditional insistence on individual initiative and responsibility. The clash between liberals and conservatives, between reformers on the left and reformers on the right, is an essential ingredient in the vitality of American life. Emotion as well as reason will always play a part in the discussion of great public issues. But when decisions have to be taken, they must be preceded by a clear-headed analysis of all the relevant facts; this is as true of the Federal Government as it is of the individual company. By their example and by their participation in these discussions, businessmen can help to remove the greatest obstacle to rational decision-making – ignorance of the facts.

Epilogue

SINCE this book was written the American economy has shown further signs of boiling over into inflation. Unemployment has continued to fall, prices have been rising, shortages of men and materials have become more widespread. President Johnson and his advisers, reluctant to take firm deflationary measures for fear of bringing the five-year-old economic advance to a halt, have been relying more heavily on persuasion to maintain price stability. There are reports of extensive, though discreet, intervention in the price decisions of businessmen, and to a lesser extent in the wage demands of unions. Adding yet another refinement to the 'guidepost' approach to business–government co-operation, the President has asked large companies voluntarily to cut back their capital investment programmes, as a contribution towards keeping the economy on an even keel.

Meanwhile the image of business has come under attack once again. General Motors has found itself at the centre of a storm over car safety. Its senior executives have reacted defensively to charges of indifference and carelessness made at a Congressional committee of investigation. (An official from the U.S. Department of Labour told the committee that the industry's profits were 'drenched in blood'.) At the same time General Motors has been found guilty by the Supreme Court of 'a classic conspiracy' to restrain competition, by attempting to prevent the sale of its cars through discount houses. The issues in this case were more complex, and the verdict more arguable, than in the great electrical conspiracy,* but the damage to the company's reputation was considerable.

No doubt both the American economy and General Motors will recover from these buffetings. The events of the past few months provide further evidence, if it is needed, that the Americans are not infallible, either in running their economy or in managing

* See page 39.

their companies. Britain is not unique in having serious economic and industrial problems to overcome.

What can a study of American experience contribute to a solution of Britain's difficulties? The most fundamental of these problems is the need to improve the competitiveness of industry, so that a larger proportion of the country's production is diverted from its present use into exports or into substitutes for imports. Some economists argue that the most effective way of achieving this result is to devalue the pound. They quote with approval the observation made by the Radcliffe Committee on the Working of the Monetary System that 'experience has revealed no other instrument as powerful as devaluation that can be used to restore competitive power'.

According to this school of thought, Government measures aimed at improving the supply side of the economy – measures to stimulate competition, provide better training for workers and managers, encourage investment in new plant and machinery, promote greater expenditure on technological research, and so on – are inevitably uncertain and long-term in their effect; they do not provide a quick enough remedy for the country's pressing balance-of-payments problem. Even a successful incomes policy, they suggest, is unlikely to alter Britain's relative position, in terms of industrial costs and export prices, decisively enough or quickly enough to bring about the improvement in competitiveness which is required.

Others are more optimistic. They think that a combination of Government measures to improve the efficiency of industry, together with direct action to reduce the balance-of-payments deficit – cutting down on overseas defence commitments, restraining overseas investment by businessmen, tinkering with the tax system to give financial incentives to exporters, temporarily curbing imports – will do the trick, without the international upheaval which would be involved in a devaluation of the pound.

Whichever view is accepted, there is no disagreement about the desirability, in principle, of long-term measures to make the supply side of the economy more efficient. The difficulty is that it is impossible to be precise or dogmatic about the contribution which any one of these measures will make to industrial efficiency and faster economic growth; the pay-off from a greater investment in, for example, management education is assumed to be large, but it cannot be accurately calculated. This is one of the reasons why it is difficult to isolate specific aspects of the American economy which have made a decisive contribution to American prosperity and hence should be borrowed for use in Britain.

Quite apart from the obvious differences between the two countries which may make such borrowing dangerous – for example, the dangers of a tough anti-merger policy in a country where a number of industries are far too fragmented in structure – it is impossible to demonstrate even for the United States that the antitrust laws have made a positive contribution to economic growth. All that can be said is that in the United States Government measures to stimulate competition, particularly in the field of price-fixing, have probably made it more difficult for firms to pass on increased costs to their customers in the form of higher prices, and thus have put more pressure on them to find ways of cutting costs. In both countries a rational assessment of the economic benefits to be derived from a vigorous anti-monopoly policy is clouded by moral and social considerations, such as the fear of bigness, which sometimes conflict with the pursuit of efficiency.

Another feature of the American economy which is often regarded as worthy of imitation in this country is the system of legally binding contracts between employers and unions. It is probably true that this system makes it easier for companies to avoid unofficial strikes, though it does not eliminate them. The handling of grievances within the plant is generally more efficient and more rational in the United States than in Britain. But the system in itself provides no ready-made solution for the profound management–union disagreements which occur from time to time in the United States as well as in Britain. The recent series of strikes in the New York newspaper industry reflects a disagreement of this kind. To make collective bargaining work is not always easy, as was shown in Chapter 6. It is possible that in Britain a change in the law would make a contribution towards more constructive labour–management relationships, but the primary factor is management's determination to put its labour relations on a sound footing.

Again, British companies look with envy at the size of the research budget administered by the American Government and its agencies. It is regarded as a technological subsidy which puts British firms at a serious disadvantage in international competition. But while the American defence and space programmes have provided an important fillip for the development of technology, it is not apparent that the resulting scientific advances have had a decisive influence, as yet, on the growth of the American economy. The U.S. Government's expenditure has indirectly created problems for certain British companies, especially in the aerospace and electronics industries, but it does not necessarily follow that these are the industries which the British Government ought to subsidize in the same way. It is generally accepted that there are certain areas of scientific research, where the benefits accruing to society are greater than the benefits for an individual firm, which should be financed by the Government. The Government, too, should use whatever buying power it possesses to stimulate technological advance. But the problem of how best to bring about a faster rate of technological innovation in civilian industry is one to which neither the American nor the British Governments have found a final solution.

The most hackneyed comparison between the two countries concerns attitudes to industrial efficiency, which, it is said, are much more favourable in the United States than in Britain. While there are important differences, shaped by history, in social attitudes towards business, their significance should not be exaggerated. There are no inherent or inherited characteristics in the British workman which make him lazier or more indisciplined than his American counterpart. Exhortation about the need for change in British attitudes is a lazy substitute for a detailed analysis of specific problems, to find out what is wrong, and what combination of policies is most likely to put it right. A study of relevant American experience – in much more detail than has been possible in this book – may well play a part in such an analysis.

Probably the most useful lessons that can be learned from America are at the level of the individual firm. Here again, if the comparison is to be helpful, it must be detailed. It is not much help to know, for example, that output per man in the American steel industry is two or three times as high as in Britain. What is needed is an item-by-item classification of the reasons for the difference – whether it lies in the size of plants (which is probably related to the size of the two home markets), or in a greater degree of mechanization (which is affected by the relative costs of capital and labour in the two countries), or in better supervision of labour, or in some other factor. This is the sort of detailed inter-firm comparison which should uncover specific opportunities for cost reduction.

Needless to say, for most British companies which want to make themselves more efficient it is not necessary to make an extended visit to the United States, or to conduct an inter-firm comparison with an American company. The steps that have to be taken to pull a company round are not usually very complex or sophisticated. For example, an 'efficiency campaign' in a typical run-down company might start with a determined effort to raise the level of competence among workpeople, supervisors and management – by starting new apprentice schemes, sending selected supervisors to outside courses, recruiting new executives with special qualifications and so on. It would also involve a strengthening of the technical side of the company and a closer attention to marketing and distribution, not merely to cut costs, but, for example, to ensure that the firm's products are priced in a way which encourages the customer to buy standard items in large volume. Most important of all, the programme would involve a clear definition of the company's objectives, both quantitatively in terms of return on capital, rate of growth, and so on and also in terms of what kind of company it wants to become in five or ten years' time, what markets it intends to supply, what technologies it aims to pursue. This would be followed by the setting of detailed objectives, both short-term and long-term, for individual managers, and by the establishment of procedures for checking each manager's performance against those objectives.

This sort of operation is going on in a large number of British companies, usually in response to economic pressures – a drop in profits – which have forced the management to take action. There are, in addition, many British companies which are already excellently managed by the best American standards and which can serve as examples for those average firms that are trying to pull themselves up into the top level.

It remains true, nevertheless, that the average standard of management is higher in the United States than in Britain. Experienced observers of both countries' industries have concluded that, as a general rule, American firms devote a more minute attention to cost reduction and profit improvement than do British firms. There is no single explanation for this phenomenon, but one important factor may be found in the description* of the idea behind the foundation of the Harvard Business School – 'that the administration of business enterprises needed to be and could be a professional matter worthy of the time and attention of learned, thoughtful, and responsible men.'

The Americans were the pioneers in the development of a professional approach to business management. Britain is gradually catching up, and has already made some progress along the road. The change in British management is apparent, not merely in the creation of new graduate business schools and in the general flowering of business studies at universities, technical colleges, and elsewhere but also in the emergence of a new generation of businessmen which has a good deal in common with America's new generation described in Chapter 11. Like their American counterparts, they are free from the traditional prejudices associated with the business community. They are pragmatic in their attitudes towards government. Their approach to business and other problems is wholly rational. They are students of the 'science' of management. They are eager to learn about, and apply, all the new tools of management – some of which, of course, have been developed in the United States.

There is clearly a connexion between the emergence of this new type of manager and the drive for efficiency which is now going

* See page 118.

on in a large number of British companies. There is encouraging evidence that a modernization of British industry and British management is in progress. It would be foolish to suppose that this transformation, by itself, will put the British economy right. But it is one of the factors which, at least in the long term, should help to bring about the increase in industrial competitiveness on which so much depends. The performance of the British economy will be greatly influenced by the efforts of those 'learned, thoughtful, and responsible men' who in Britain, as in the United States, are increasingly tending to fill the top management posts in industry.

A note on further reading

Two useful and comprehensive books on the relationship between government and industry are M. Fainsod, L. Gordon, J. C. Pala-mountain, *Government and the American Economy* (Norton, New York, 1959); and V. A. Mund, *Government and Business* (Harper & Brothers, New York, 1950). A brief introduction to the subject is provided by Richard Caves, *American Industry, Structure, Conduct and Performance* (Prentice-Hall, Foundations of Modern Economics Series, N.J., 1964).

On the role of the corporation in the American economy a valuable collection of essays is *The Corporation in Modern Society*, edited by E. S. Mason (Harvard University Press, 1959). See also A. A. Berle, *The American Economic Republic* (Harcourt Brace, New York, 1963); Thomas C. Cochran, *The American Business System, A Historical Perspective* (Harvard University Press, 1957); and A. D. H. Kaplan, *Big Enterprise in a Competitive System* (Brookings Institution, Washington D.C., 1954).

For a critical account of government regulation see Marver H. Bernstein, *Regulating Business by Independent Commissions* (Princeton University Press, 1955). On the problems of the railways see *Technological Change and the Future of the Railways* (Conference conducted by the Transportation Center at Northwestern University in January, 1961). A general survey of Government transport policy is contained in *Report on National Transportation Policy prepared for the Interstate Commerce Committee of the U.S. Senate* (Government Printing Office, January 1961). See also *Transportation Renaissance, the Annals of the American Academy of Political and Social Science* (Philadelphia, 1963). The growth of the nuclear power industry and the impact of the Federal Government is described in Philip Mullenbach, *Civilian Nuclear Power* (Twentieth Century Fund, New York, 1959).

From the vast literature on the promotion of competition the following books are suggested: Carl Kaysen and Donald Turner, *Antitrust Policy* (Harvard University Press, 1959); T. J. Kreps, *An Evaluation of Antitrust Policy* (Study Paper No. 22, Joint Economic Committee of Congress, Government Printing Office, 1960); E. S. Mason, *Economic Concentration and the Monopoly Problem* (Harvard University Press, 1957); and *Report of the Attorney General's National Committee to Study the Antitrust Laws* (Government Printing Office, 1955).

Recent trends in merger activity are analysed in *Mergers and Super-concentration, a staff report by the House Small Business Committee* (Government Printing Office, 1962). On price competition see National Bureau of Economic Research, *Business Concentration and Price Policy* (Princeton University Press, 1955); A. D. H. Kaplan, J. B. Dirlam, R. F. Lanzilotti, *Pricing in Big Business* (Brookings Institution, Washington D.C., 1958); and Gardiner C. Means, *Pricing Power and the Public Interest, A Study based on Steel* (Harper & Brothers, New York, 1962). Means' book draws heavily on the study of 'administered prices' in the steel industry conducted by Senator Kefauver's Subcommittee on Antitrust and Monopoly.

A good collection of essays on the major American industries is *The Structure of American Industry*, edited by Walter Adams (Macmillan, New York, 1957). See also J. S. Bain, *Barriers to New Competition* (Harvard University Press, 1956); J. W. Markham, *Competition in the Rayon Industry* (Harvard University Press, 1952); J. W. McKie, *Tin Cans and Tin Plate* (Harvard University Press, 1957); *Staff Report to the Federal Trade Commission, Economic Inquiry into Food Marketing* (Part 1, January 1960, Part 2, December 1962, Government Printing Office).

A lively account of the role of shareholders is J. A. Livingston, *The American Stockholder* (Collier Books, New York, 1963). See also *The Insiders, A Stockholder's Guide to Wall Street*, by T. A. Wise and the Editors of *Fortune* (Doubleday, New York, 1962). The growth of institutional investors is analysed in two books by A. A. Berle, *The Twentieth Century Capitalist Revolution* (Harcourt Brace, New York, 1954) and *Power Without Property* (Harcourt Brace, New York, 1959). For a comprehensive account of the workings of the stock exchanges, see *Report of Special Study of Securities Markets of the Securities and Exchange Commission* (Government Printing Office, Washington, 1963).

The classic work on the relationship between unions and management is S. H. Slichter, J. J. Healy, Robert Livernash, *The Impact of Collective Bargaining on Management* (Brookings Institution, Washington D.C., 1960). See also Clark Kerr, *Labor and Management in Industrial Society* (Doubleday Anchor, New York, 1964); Robert M. Macdonald, *Collective Bargaining in the Automobile Industry* (Yale University Press, 1963); and *The Public Interest in National Labor Policy*, by an Independent Study Group (Committee for Economic Development, New York, 1961). Pessimistic accounts of the prospects facing the labour movement are given in Solomon Barkin, *The Decline of the Labor Movement* (A Report to the Center for the Study of Democratic Institutions, Santa Barbara, California, 1961); and *The Crisis in the American Trade Union Movement*, *Annals of the American Academy of Political and Social Science* (Philadelphia, November 1963). Some examples of progress in adapting the institution of collective bargaining are given in G. G. Somers, E. L. Cushman, N. Weinberg, *Adjusting to Technological Change* (Harper & Row, New York, 1963). B. C. Roberts, *Unions in America, A British View* (Princeton University, 1959), compares the development and organization of British and American trade unions.

Two important studies of business education are R. A. Gordon and J. E. Howell, *Higher Education for Business* (Columbia University Press, New York, 1959); and Frank Pierson, *The Education of American Businessmen*. See also Melvin Anshen and G. L. Bach, *Management and Corporations 1985* (McGraw-Hill, New York, 1960). An account of budgeting and planning techniques within the individual company is provided by Neil W. Chamberlain, *The Firm: Micro-Economic Planning and Action* (McGraw-Hill, New York, 1963). An important historical study of the administration of large companies, with special reference to Du Pont, General Motors, Standard Oil (New Jersey), and Sears Roebuck, is Alfred D. Chandler, *Strategy and Structure* (The M.I.T. Press, 1962).

For a critical account of American overseas investment, chiefly in the developing countries, see Richard D. Robinson, *International Business Policy* (Holt, Rinehart & Winston, New York, 1964). See also W. Friedman and G. Kalmanoff, *Joint International Business Ventures* (Columbia University Press, New York, 1961). On the strategy of overseas investment see Gilbert Clee and Alfred di Scipio, 'Creating a World Enterprise' (*Harvard Business Review*, November–December 1959).

On research and technological advance see National Bureau of Economic Research, *The Rate and Direction of Inventive Activity* (Princeton University Press, 1962); *Patterns and Problems of Technical Innovation in American Industry*, Report to National Science Foundation (U.S. Department of Commerce, September 1963); *Problems of Innovation in American Industry* (U.S. Department of Commerce, May 1963); *The Role and Effect of Technology in the Nation's Economy*, *Hearings before a subcommittee of the Select Committee on Small Business, U.S. Senate* (Government Printing Office, 1963); and *Federal*

Research and Development Programs, Hearings before the Select Committee on Government Research, House of Representatives (Government Printing Office, 1963).

On economic growth the annual *Economic Report of the President*, which is published in January of each year and which contains the much longer Annual Report of the Council of Economic Advisers, is the best guide to Government policy. The Council's 1962 Report provides a lucid account of the Kennedy Administration's attitude to economic growth, while that of 1964 contains a thorough analysis of the Council's views on unemployment. See also Edward F. Denison, *The Sources of Economic Growth in the United States* (Committee for Economic Development, New York, 1962); Gunnar Myrdal, *Challenge to Affluence* (Pantheon Books, New York, 1962); and Albert T. Sommers, *The Economic Environment of the Middle Sixties* (National Industrial Conference Board, New York, September 1964). On manpower policy see *Manpower Policy and Programmes in the United States* (Organization for Economic Cooperation and Development, Paris, 1964); and *Unemployment and the American Economy*, edited by Arthur M. Ross (John Wiley, New York, 1964). The latter contains a useful comparison of American and European approaches to manpower problems.

On business ideology see *The Business Establishment*, edited by Earl F. Cheit (John Wiley, New York, 1964); John R. Bunting, *The Hidden Face of Free Enterprise* (McGraw-Hill, New York, 1964); and F. X. Sutton, S. E. Harris, Carl Kaysen, James Tobin, *The American Business Creed* (Harvard University Press, 1956).

Notes

Chapter 1

1. See H. J. Habbakuk, *American and British Technology in the Nine-teenth Century* (Cambridge University Press, 1962).
2. Quoted in Habbakuk, op. cit., p. 112.
3. An example of this approach to economic history is *The Enter-prising Americans*, by John Chamberlain (Harper Colophon Books, New York, 1962).
4. The phrase is used by Thurman Arnold in *The Folklore of Capi-talism* (Yale University Press, 1936).

Chapter 2

1. See Walter Adams and Horace Gray, *Monopoly in America* (Mac-millan, New York, 1955), Ch. VI.
2. For a description of this process, see J. Roger Morison and Richard F. Neuschel, 'The Second Squeeze on Profits', *Harvard Business Review*, July–August 1962.
3. George Stocking, quoted in Walter Adams, *The Structure of Ameri-can Industry* (Macmillan, New York, 1957), p. 190. The com-ments were based on a study of the company by Ford, Bacon & Davis, engineering consultants.
4. Donald Kircher, 'Now the Transnational Enterprise', *Harvard Business Review*, March–April 1964, p. 7.
5. Quoted in W. H. Bingham and D. L. Yunich, 'Retail Reorganiza-tion', *Harvard Business Review*, July–August 1965, p. 132.
6. 'Opportunities to improve relations between chains and manu-facturers', commissioned by National Association of Food Chains (October 1962).
7. 'The Economics of Food Distributors', commissioned by General Foods (October 1963).

Chapter 3

1. E. S. Mason, *Economic Concentration and the Monopoly Problem* (Harvard University Press, 1957), p. 178.
2. Dale Hathaway, *Government and Agriculture* (Macmillan, New York, 1963), p. 156.
3. A. D. H. Kaplan, J. Dirlam and R. Lanzilotti, *Pricing in Big Busi-ness* (Brookings Institution, 1958), p. 168.

4. See Norman Collins and Lee Preston, 'The Size Structure of the Largest Industrial Firms 1909–58', *American Economic Review*, December 1961.

5. See Corwin Edwards, *The Price Discrimination Law* (Brookings Institution, 1959).

6. Lawrence Litchfield Jr, chairman of Alcoa, address before National Industrial Conference Board, 5 March 1964.

7. For an assessment of this programme, see Samuel Hayes and Donald Woods, 'Are S.B.I.C.'s doing their job?', *Harvard Business Review*, March–April 1963.

8. M. A. Adelman, address before National Industrial Conference Board, 5 March 1964.

Chapter 4

1. *Rationale of Federal Transportation Policy* (U.S. Department of Commerce, April 1960), p. 5.

2. ibid., p. 5.

3. See A. R. Ferguson *et al.*, *The Economic Value of the U.S. Merchant Marine* (Northwestern University, 1961).

4. *Civilian Nuclear Power, a Report to the President* (Atomic Energy Commission, 1962), p. 8.

5. F. R. Kappel, *Vitality in a Business Enterprise* (McGraw-Hill, New York, 1960), p. 48.

Chapter 5

1. A. A. Berle, *Economic Power and the Free Society* (Center for the Study of Democratic Institutions, Santa Barbara, California, 1959), p. 9.

2. Robert G. Donnelley, 'The Family Business', *Harvard Business Review*, July–August 1964.

3. Ernest Dale, 'Management Must be Made Accountable', *Harvard Business Review*, March–April 1960. See also the same author's *The Great Organizers* (McGraw-Hill, New York, 1961).

4. See Arch Patton, 'Executive Compensation in 1970', *Harvard Business Review*, September–October 1964.

5. Berle, op. cit., p. 7.

6. Robert J. Lampmann, *The Share of Top Wealth-holders in National Wealth* (Princeton University Press, 1962), p. 208.

7. Abram Chayes in *The Corporation in Modern Society*, edited by E. S. Mason (Harvard University Press, 1959), p. 40.

8. Address by Sidney Homer to Boston Economic Club, 15 April 1964.
9. Address by Robert F. Carney, Chairman of Foote, Cone & Belding, to New York Society of Security Analysts, 30 December 1963.
10. *Forbes Magazine*, 15 September 1963.

Chapter 6

1. *Labor looks at labor* (Center for the Study of Democratic Institutions, Santa Barbara, California, 1963), p. 16.
2. See Robert M. Macdonald, *Collective Bargaining in the Automobile Industry* (Yale University Press, 1963), Chapters VI and VII.
3. Herbert R. Northrup, 'The Case for Boulwarism', *Harvard Business Review*, September–October 1963.
4. Clark Kerr, *Labor and Management in Industrial Society* (Doubleday Anchor, New York, 1964), p. 276.
5. Solomon Barkin, *The Decline of the Labor Movement* (a report to the Center for the Study of Democratic Institutions, Santa Barbara, California, 1961), p. 5.
6. See Jack Stieber, Walter Oberer, Michael Harrington, *Democracy and Public Review* (Center for the Study of Democratic Institutions, Santa Barbara, California, 1960).
7. *Labor looks at labor* (op. cit.), p. 24.
8. Neil Chamberlain in *The Corporation in Modern Society*, edited by E. S. Mason (Harvard University Press, 1959), p. 32.
9. *The Public Interest in National Labor Policy* (Committee for Economic Development, New York, 1961), p. 32.

Chapter 7

1. Alfred P. Sloan, *My Years with General Motors* (Doubleday, New York, 1964; Sidgwick Jackson, London, 1965), p. 55.
2. ibid., p. 144.
3. See William H. Mylander, 'Management by Executive Committee', *Harvard Business Review*, May–June 1955.
4. Sloan, op. cit., p. 433. See also Harold A. Wolff, 'The Great G.M. Mystery', *Harvard Business Review*, September–October 1964.
5. Stanley F. Teele in foreword to *And Mark an Era, The Story of the Harvard Business School*, by Melvin T. Copeland (Little, Brown, Boston, 1958).

6. R. A. Gordon and J. E. Howell, *Higher Education for Business* (Columbia University Press, New York, 1959); and Frank Pierson, *The Education of American Businessmen.*

7. Herbert Simon in *Management and Corporations 1985*, edited by Melvin Anshen and George L. Bach (McGraw-Hill, New York, 1960).

8. Harold J. Leavitt and Thomas L. Whisler, 'Management in the 1980's', *Harvard Business Review*, November–December 1958.

9. Melvin Anshen, 'Executive Development: In-Company vs University Programs', *Harvard Business Review*, September–October 1954.

10. See *Preparation for Business Leadership* (Graduate School of Business Administration, University of Michigan, 1964).

11. The Edsel affair is discussed by John Brooks in *The Fate of the Edsel and Other Business Adventures* (Harper & Row, New York, 1963).

Chapter 8

1. See Alfred P. Sloan, *My Years with General Motors* (Doubleday, New York, 1964; Sidgwick Jackson, London, 1965), Ch. 18.

2. Wolfgang Friedmann and George Kalmanoff (editors), *Joint International Business Ventures* (Columbia University Press, 1961), p. 299.

3. Gilbert Clee and Wilbur Sachtjen, 'Organizing a Worldwide Business', *Harvard Business Review*, November–December 1964, p. 67.

4. ibid., p. 63.

Chapter 9

1. Yale Brozen, 'The Future of Industrial Research', *Journal of Business*, October 1961.

2. Carl Stover, *The Government of Science* (Center for the Study of Democratic Institutions, Santa Barbara, California, 1962), p. 15.

3. See the report by Arthur D. Little, *Strategies for Survival in the Aerospace Industry*, 1964.

4. See James Mahar and Dean Coddington, 'The Scientific Complex', *Harvard Business Review*, January–February 1965.

5. See Lawrence Lessing, 'The 400 m.p.h. Passenger Train', *Fortune Magazine*, April 1965.

6. *Patterns and Problems of Technical Innovation in American Industry,*

report by Arthur D. Little to National Science Foundation (Department of Commerce, September 1963), p. 197.

7. See Melville Hodge, 'Rate Your Company's Research Productivity', *Harvard Business Review*, November–December 1963.

8. *Patterns and Problems* (op. cit.), p. 181.

Chapter 10

1. *Economic Report of the President, together with annual report of the Council of Economic Advisers* (Government Printing Office, January 1962), p. 139.

2. op. cit., p. 171.

3. op. cit., Ch. 4.

4. *Economic Report of the President, together with annual report of the Council of Economic Advisers* (Government Printing Office, January 1964), p. 120.

5. Thomas J. Watson, *A Business and Its Beliefs* (McGraw-Hill, New York, 1963), p. 101.

6. *Manpower Report of the President* (Government Printing Office, March 1964), p. 71.

7. *Manpower Policy and Programmes in the United States* (O.E.C.D., Paris, 1964), p. 74.

8. *Economic Report of the President, together with annual report of the Council of Economic Advisers* (Government Printing Office, January 1964), p. 184.

9. *Technological Trends in thirty-six Major American Industries, A Study prepared for the President's Committee on Labor-Management Policy* (U.S. Department of Labor, 1964).

10. V. R. Fuchs, *Productivity Trends in the Goods and Service Sectors 1929–61* (Columbia University Press, 1964).

11. Garth Mangum in *Monthly Labor Review*, May, 1965.

12. *Economic Report of the President, together with annual report of the Council of Economic Advisers* (Government Printing Office, January 1962), p. 128.

13. E. S. Mason in *American Economic Review*, March 1963.

14. W. W. Leontief, 'Proposal for better business forecasting', *Harvard Business Review*, November–December 1964.

Chapter 11

1. Quoted by Abram Chayes in *The Corporation in Modern Society*, edited by E. S. Mason (Harvard University Press, 1959), p. 27.

2. Lawrence G. Lavengood, 'American Business and the Piety of Profits', *Harvard Business Review*, November–December 1959, p. 55.
3. In *New York Herald Tribune*, 5 January 1964.
4. Robert Heilbroner, in *The Business Establishment*, edited by Earl F. Cheit (John Wiley, New York, 1964), p. 36.
5. Thomas J. Watson, *A Business and Its Beliefs* (McGraw-Hill, New York, 1963), p. 99.

Index

Index

*Some other books published by Penguins
are described on the following pages.*

Economic Planning and Democracy

Firmin Oulès

The currents of economic planning and democratic freedom run counter. Hence one of our acutest dilemmas.

Professor Oulès, leader of 'The New Lausanne School' of economists, faces this difficulty squarely in a new Pelican in which he effectively 'demystifies' the economic complex of Western Europe, laying bare the forces which determine the array of facts and figures we call economics. His examination is both honest and intelligent, and he comments forcefully on the anti-democratic trend of 'indicative planning', as practised notably in France.

As an alternative Professor Oulès makes his own recommendation. It is for 'planning by enlightenment' – a concept which combines budgetary co-ordination, at the national level, with the systematic provision of enough data for industry, finance, commerce, and labour to act rationally yet freely.

Economic Planning and Democracy is at once a brilliantly clear exposition of the material realities of trade and industry and a constructive solution of a problem which is today admitted by most politicians and economists.

Into Work

Michael Carter

The more we educate, it seems, the vaguer school leavers are becoming about their future careers. They wander unarmed into the jungle of industrial society: to the tiger they are merely fodder.

This Pelican Original is the work of a sociologist who has specialized in education and delinquency. It stresses the present inadequacies in the passage leading from school to work, particularly for the thousands educated in secondary modern schools. Too often family life exerts a stultifying pressure, and schools, colleges, and the Youth Employment Service offer too little guidance.

Michael Carter's study of such shortcomings, and of the whole field of training for work, poses fundamental questions. What is the purpose of education? Can it only be a talent-broker for an economic system, or might it produce men and women capable of developing their own abilities and of shaping rather than being shaped by society?

How, in other words, can we best prepare young people for the day when they go 'into work'?

Britain and the World Economy

J. M. Livingstone

In the world's market-place every country keeps a stall and every country goes shopping. The result – in currency, credit, and kind – is a network of transactions as intricate and alive as a printed circuit.

Britain and the World Economy is a short, readable survey of the part played by one country in this world network. Britain, partly by necessity, partly by choice, plays a variety of economic roles in the world and J. M. Livingstone emphasizes the country's growing dependence on events abroad in this examination of her contributions as an international banker operating the sterling system; as the leader of a still powerful Commonwealth; as a force in a revitalized Europe; as a world trader; and as a 'have' with responsibilities towards the 'have-nots'.

Attitudes in British Management

A.P.E.P. Report

Efficient industry is in the hands of the managers. With this in mind the research staff of P.E.P. recently interviewed 300 senior executives in industries ranging from domestic appliances to shipbuilding. They wanted to find out which industrial practices 'appeared to be conducive to growth'. *Attitudes in British Management* is the report of their findings.

Managers, it appears, fall naturally into two categories: 'thrusters' and 'sleepers' ... those who meet problems as challenges and those who allow their firms to stagnate. Many of the reasons for success or failure are suggested by the verbatim answers given to P.E.P.'s questions by men actively involved in the conduct of industry.

If Britain is to revitalize her economy, most of the answers are here. Can they be applied?

(This is the first of a new Pelican sub-series entitled 'Business and Administration', under the general editorship of Colin McIver. This P.E.P. report was written by Anthony Gater, David Insull, Harold Lind, and Peter Seglow, of the research staff.)

The Consumer Society:

A HISTORY OF AMERICAN CAPITALISM

Peter d'A. Jones

How did America get rich? How has wealth affected her people and her culture? What is the future of her economy likely to be? These are some of the questions dealt with in this dynamic survey of the economic, social and political forces that have made America the richest country the world has ever known.

Skilfully blending economic theory and narrative history, the author explains those elements of colonial society that formed the basis for the country's economic growth, the factors which allowed it to progress from an agricultural economy to an industrial one from 1860 to 1920 and finally the emergence of today's consumer capitalism. He stresses his view throughout that social democracy, mobility and opportunity are the historical foundations of America's wealth, and argues that so long as the American people preserve an open society their wealth will continue to grow.

The Economic History of
World Population

Carlo M. Cipolla

This book presents a global view of the demographic and economic development of mankind.

Professor Cipolla has deliberately adopted a new point of view and has tried to trace the history of the great trends in population and wealth which have affected mankind as a whole.

Among the massive problems that face the human race the author emphasizes the demographic explosion, the economic backwardness of vast areas, the spread of industrial revolution and of technical knowledge. Whilst the theoretical approach can help our analysis of these problems, Professor Cipolla believes that they can only be wholly grasped and solved when they are studied in their full historical perspective.